The Bible Period by Period

A Manual for the Study of the
Bible by Periods

Josiah Blake Tidwell

The Bible Period by Period: A Manual for the Study of the Bible by Periods

Copyright © 2018 Indo-European Publishing

The present edition is a reproduction of previous publication of this work. Minor typographical errors may have been corrected without note, however, for an authentic reading experience the spelling, punctuation, and capitalization have been retained from the original text.

ISBN: 978-1-60444-843-6

TABLE OF CONTENTS

Chapter I

Problems solved. Creation of man. Man's hope and occupation. The temptation. The fall and punishment. The hope offered. Teachings of the story. Topics for discussion.

Chapter II

Cain and Abel. Cain and Seth, two races. The great wickedness. Noah God's chosen man. The Ark. The flood. The sacrifice and rainbow covenant. Confirmation of tradition and geology. Teachings of the period. Topics for discussion.

Chapter III

Noah's shame and prophecy. The Tower of Babel. The location of this tower. Specific purpose of the tower. Traditions of such a tower. The civilization of the ancient world. Two great empires of antiquity. Language and literature. Motive of their civilization. Lessons of the period. Topics for discussion.

Chapter IV

Events of the period. Purpose of the narrative. Conditions of the times. Confirmations of Biblical records. Experiences of Abraham. The character of Abraham. The character and career of Isaac. Stories about Jacob. Stories about Joseph. Death of Jacob and Joseph. Social and religious conditions of the times. The book of Job. Lessons of the period. Topics for discussion.

Chapter V

Israel in Egypt. Moses the deliverer. The great deliverance. Crossing the Red Sea. Journey to Sinai. Lessons of the period. Topics.

Chapter VI

Mount Sinai. The Sinaitic covenant. Purpose of the Mosaic Law. Several parts of the law. Journey to Kadesh-Barnea. Twelve spies. Period lessons. Topics for discussion.

Chapter VII

The pathos of the forty years. Events of the forty years' wandering. Final scenes at Kadesh. From Kadesh to Jordan. Prophecies of Balaam. Last acts of Moses. Last scene on Moab.

Significance of the work of Moses. Lessons of the period. Topics for discussion. .

Chapter VIII

The facts of history recorded. The story in three parts. The land of Canaan. Crossing Jordan and fall of Jericho. The complete conquest of Canaan. Cruelty to the Canaanites. Character and work of Joshua. Period lessons. Topics for discussion.

Chapter IX

Characteristics of tie times. The Judges. Ruth the Moabite. Other nations. Outline of the narrative. Ethical and religious standards. Period lessons. Topics for discussion.

Chapter X

Demand for a king. The principle of the kingdom. Saul, the first king. Saul's great achievements. Saul's decline. Period lessons. Topics for discussion.

Chapter XI

His reign over Judah. Reign over all Israel. His great sin and its bitter consequences. David's inspiring career. His last days. Psalms. Period lessons. Topics for discussion.

Chapter XII

Riddle of Solomon's character. His policies. Solomon's building enterprises. Solomon's writings. Nations surrounding Israel. Evidences of national decay. Period lessons. Topics for discussion.

Chapter XIII

The division of the kingdom. Comparison of the two kingdoms. Kings of the Northern kingdom. Kings of Judah. Important events in the history of Israel. Principal events in the history of Judah. Relation between the two kingdoms. Messages of the prophets of this period. Period lessons. Topics for discussion.

Chapter XIV

The kings of the period. Principal events of the period. Prophets of the period and their messages. Teachings of the period. False prophets. Great religious revivals of this period. Wealth and luxury. Contemporary nations. Period lessons. Topics for discussion.

Chapter XV

The ten tribes lost. Judah led into captivity. The period of the captivity. The fugitives in Egypt. Exiles in Babylon. The prophets of the exile. Benefits of the captivity. Lessons of the period. Topics for discussion.

Chapter XVI

Scripture analysis. Predictions of the return. Rise of the Persian Power. The Decree of Cyrus. Three Expeditions to Jerusalem. Prophecy of Haggai and Zechariah. Prophecy of Malachi. Story of Esther. Synagogues and Synagogue worship. Significance of the period. Period lessons. Topics for discussion.

Chapter XVII

The close of Old Testament History. Persian period. Under the rule of Greek kings. Period of independence. The Roman period. Entire period. End of the Period. Topics for discussion.

Chapter XVIII

The story of the period. The childhood and youth of Jesus. The beginnings of Christ's Ministry. Early Judean ministry. Galilean

Ministry. Perean Ministry. Final Ministry in Jerusalem. The forty days. Teaching of the period. Topics for discussion.

Chapter XIX

The Book of Acts. Principal events of the period. Organization and control of the early church. Persecutions of the church. Growth and influence. Extension of the Gospel to the Gentiles. Teachings of the period. Topics for discussion.

Chapter XX

The changed situation. The divine call. Time and extent of Paul's journeys. First missionary journey. Second missionary journey. Third missionary journey. At Jerusalem. At Caesarea. Paul at Rome. Epistles of this period. Lessons of the period. Topics for discussion.

Chapter XXI

The period of history. Destruction of Jerusalem. From A. D. 70 to A.D. 100. Literature of the period. Death of John and end of scripture history. Period lessons. Topics for discussion.

INTRODUCTION

(Pastor Geo. W. Truett.)

In offering to the public this little book The Bible Period By Period, Dr. Tidwell is making another contribution to the cause of Bible study. He has already published Some Introductory Bible Studies, An Outline for the Study of the Life of Christ, and The Bible Book By Book.

All of these have been well received. The last named formed a part of a definite plan for the study of the sacred Scripture which is carried forward in this volume.

The fact that the first edition of The Bible Book By Book has practically all been sold before the end of the second year since its publication, is sufficient proof of its popularity and of its value to Bible students. It has been adopted for study in a number of colleges and academies and is in use as a text book in a number of women's societies and Sunday School classes.

The author, as teacher of Bible in Baylor University, has tried out the studies he offers and has had a splendid opportunity to select what has proven valuable. He teaches a larger number of young preachers than any similar instructor in the whole of the Southland, and also many Sunday School Teachers and other Christian workers. He can, therefore, offer the best.

Dr. Tidwell accepts, without question, the inspiration and authoritativeness of the Bible as the Word of God. He believes in directing the student in the study of the Bible itself rather than having him study about it. His hooks are, therefore, more in the nature of outlines or guides than of discussions. He gives the pupil a clue to the study and says only enough to create a zest for truth such as will lead to a thorough investigation of the subject in hand.

In this volume, as its title would indicate, the whole Bible has been divided into periods and main facts and characteristics of each is studied. There are twenty-one periods forming the basis for as many chapters.

The plan is to discuss in the beginning of each chapter the most striking events of the period, Giving such outlines of the contents and principal events of the period as will make the whole period stand out so that the student may comprehend it at a glance. This is very brief but most comprehensive.

In the next place the lessons and teachings of the period are suggested. The author sets forth in tabular form the great teaching found in the Scripture events, both in their value to the Hebrews and in their permanent value to all people and for all times.

In the case of the poetical and prophetic books, suggestions for their study are given in the chapter on the period in which each book and the facts it records occurred. At the close of each chapter there is given a large number of topics for study and discussion. For the most part these topics require the searching of the Scripture itself and, if properly followed, will give the student a splendid knowledge of the contents of the Scripture of the period.

This book when completed in our Sunday Schools will, if done under the direction of the author, be given credit in Baylor University as college entrance. Our Sunday School workers would do well to organize classes of young men and women in the study of this book. In this way they would not only help these young people in Bible study but would tie them all to our great school at Baylor and make it possible for them to get credit for it when they attend provided they need it to get into the college. There ought to be hundreds of such classes in Texas.

Every Sunday School teacher and woman worker would do himself or herself a valuable service by securing and studying a copy of this new book. And it is also to be hoped that many of our women's societies will adopt it for their Bible study.

Let our pastors buy this book for themselves and bring it to the attention of their people. For the people of today, as of old, are perishing from a lack of Bible knowledge. The one unceasing effort that should be constantly and whole heartedly put forth by every Christian leader in every realm is to get the people to read and to know the Holy Scripture. Dr. Tidwell's book will greatly help in such effort.

First Baptist Church, Dallas, Texas.

CHAPTER I

From The Creation to The Fall.

Gen. Chs. 1-3

Problems Solved. This simple narrative solves some of the great problems about which philosophers have speculated and before which scientists have stood baffled. Every child of the human race has asked, "What is the origin of the material world, what is the origin of life, and what is the origin of sin?" In general the philosophers held (and most of what science says concerning these matters is not science but speculative philosophy) that matter was eternal and simply asked how it came to its present state. One group, the materialists, held that an active principle inherent in the matter working through long ages, brought about the present state of things. Another group, the pantheists, held that every thing emanated from a common divine substance, working everywhere in nature. But this brief story lets at rest all this inquiry. It informs us that matter was not eternal nor did it come into existence by chance, but it was created out of nothing by our eternal God. The story incidentally sets forth the majesty and glory of God and man's dependence upon and his obligation to God. It also explains the origin of sin and of all man's ills and death.

Creation of Man. The Story of the preparation of a residence for man is told in five brief paragraphs. For concision, picturesqueness and concreteness, this narrative is not excelled in all literature. It shows how God acting as a creating Spirit through six successive periods of light and darkness prepared the world and put man in it. In the matter of the creation of man the presence and activity of Jehovah is especially emphasized. He shaped the body out of the dust of the earth and breathed into the nostrils of that human form that which made him become a living soul. It was the breath of God that gave life to man and hence he will return again to dust when that breath is withdrawn. Concerning the creation of woman it is better to admit that her creation was supernatural just as was man's. Her creation was to provide for man a helpful companionship so that his development and happiness might be complete. Her creation out of a part of man's body and to meet an inborn need provides the eternal grounds of marriage and the basis upon which they are in marriage to become one flesh and by reason of which man must "love his wife as his own flesh." Man is created in the image of God and like the Creator has intelligence and will and is given authority to rule over the earth.

Man's Home and Occupation. No sooner was man created than was planted in the far distant east a garden that should be to him a home and provide therein for his physical and spiritual needs. Where that garden was located is not known with certainty. Occupation was, however, provided so that he might exercise and develop each part of his nature. He exercised his mind in naming the animals and in some way the tree of good and evil was destined to be for his blessing. His soul had fellowship with Eve his helpmate and God his creator. This garden also had in it a life-giving tree that gave them the possibility of enjoying an endless life should they remain near it and continue to eat its fruit.

The Temptation. The study proceeds on the basis that there was already a race of fallen beings in the universe. Satan was the chief of these and had the mysterious power of tempting others to follow him. He assumed the form of a serpent-a creature least likely to be suspected and thereby deceived Eve the weaker. The temptation had several elements: (1) The talking serpent was to her in the nature of a miracle; (2) Eve had not heard the command of God herself (it was given before her creation) but had learned it from Adam. The devil therefore raised a doubt as to whether God really forbade it; (3) The question implies a doubt concerning the goodness and wisdom of God; (4) It appeals to the lust of flesh, to the pride of the eye and to the pride of life. It was beautiful, good for food, and to make her wise even like God; (5) In this appeal to curiosity there is an implied dare; (6) She was told that she had a mistaken idea of the penalty-that she should "not surely die."

In all this it will be noted that the temptation was to fall upward. All the motives-the satisfaction of natural appetite, the desire for knowledge and power and the love for beauty were in themselves worthy. The temptation was to better herself. Such it is always. Adam was not directly approached, but he willfully disobeyed without being beguiled as was the woman. The chief blame, therefore, fell upon him.

The Fall and Punishment. The fearful consequences of their sin are felt at once. They are changed so that they are conscious of guilt and endeavor to hide themselves from Jehovah. Thus they acknowledge their unfitness for fellowship with Him. Their soul having lost communion with God, they become corrupt. This is spiritual death. They were banished from the garden and forced to struggle for food. Their bodies became subject to pain and death by separation from the animating spirit. They could not longer eat of the life-giving tree of the garden. The earth was cursed so that instead of ministering to man's pleasure and support, it would produce much to his hurt. The woman in her unredeemed state was to be in subordination to her husband. The sad story of downtrodden women in heathen lands of all times since then, and even today wherever Christ is not known, tells something of the awful results of her sin.

The Hope Offered. The gloom of this sad story of their punishment was relieved by an element of hope. The man and his wife are not beyond the pale of God's love. There is given a promise (3:15) which assures the coming of one, who would contend with the tempter and would finally crush his head and repair the damage of the Fall. All of the rest of the Bible unfolds the plan and work of God in fulfilling this promise. There is beginning with Cain and Abel and running through the entire scripture a record of the conflict caused by the enmity between the seed of woman and that of her seducer. This conflict is to end when Christ the "seed of the woman" shall return to reign and shall cast his adversary into the bottomless pit. Along with this promise he also provided for them garments of the skins of animals such as were suited to their new and hostile environment and in which most writers find a suggestion of the covering of righteousness that comes to guilty sinners through the death of Jesus. Then too there was erected at the east of the garden an alter of worship not unlike that provided in connection with the Tabernacle later and where God dwelt in mercy and could be approached. Here was opened up a way by which they might after being forgiven again have a right to the tree of life and live forever.

Some Teachings of this Story. Back of this story are many truths worthy of most careful study. They constitute the basal facts of all history and religion. The following are put down as among the most vital: (1) Back of all nature is a personal Creator and Ruler who has the

3

tenderest solicitude and care for man, as the highest product of his creation. (2) There was an orderly progress in creation from the more simple and less important to the most complex and most important. (3) All things were made for man and his comfort. (4) Marriage is a sacred obligation growing out of the very character of man and woman who were made for each other and each can, therefore, meet the deepest needs of the other. (5) Sin does not originate in God but in man's yielding to his baser instead of his nobler and diviner motives. (6) Sin as a cause brings its own punishment, the worst of which is the separation of the individual from harmonious relations with God, which is spiritual death.

For Study and Discussion. (1) The condition of the material universe when God began to prepare it for man's abode. (2) The six creative days or periods and what was created in each. (3) The special emphasis upon the presence and activity of God in the creation of man and woman. (4) The divine interest in and preparation for the happiness of man. (5) The home prepared for them. (6) The lessons about marriage, its purpose, basis, etc. (7) The law and place of testing in the formation of character. (8) The ills of life that are the results of some one's sin. (9) The nature and results of the curse upon the man, upon the woman, upon the tempter. (10) God's care for man after the Fall and the provisions for his recovery. (11) The revelation of God made by these three chapters. (12) The image of God in man..

CHAPTER II

From the Fall to the Flood.

Gen. Chs. 4-8.

Cain and Abel. These two, who are apparently the oldest children of the first pair, were no doubt born soon after the expulsion from the garden. One tilled the soil and the other was a shepherd. They each appear to have been attentive to worship. Their offerings, however, were very different and no doubt revealed a difference of spirit. The superiority of Abel's offering was in the faith in which it was made (Heb. 11:4), meaning perhaps that he relied upon the promise of God and that he apprehended the truth that without shedding of blood there is no remission. (Heb. 12:24).

Because God granted to Abel a token of acceptance of his offering and failed to grant a like token to Cain, the latter became jealous and finally slew his brother. Thus early did Adam and Eve begin to reap the effects of sin. The record, in kindness to them, makes no mention of the great sorrow that must have come to them as they saw their second son murdered by their first-born. These two sons represent two types running through all the Bible and indeed through all history-the unchecked power of evil and the triumph of faith. They represent two types of religion, one of faith and the other of works. Then as in all succeeding ages the true worshipers were persecuted by false worshipers.

God showed his mercy to Cain whom he sent away from the place of worship at the east of the garden by putting upon him the divine mark so that no one should destroy him. He also allowed him to prosper and it was through his descendants that civilization began to show itself.

Cain and Seth-Two Races. Another son was born to Adam named Seth. Probably others have been born since the death of Abel but none of a like spirit to Abel and hence none worthy to become the head of a spiritual branch of mankind. Cain's descendants applied themselves to the arts and to manufactures, to the building of cities and the making

5

those things that furnish earthly comfort, while the descendants of Seth, were selected to be the instruments of religious uplift and to have communion with Jehovah. Through inter-marriage with the descendants of Cain, however, the generation of Seth was corrupted. This led to a period of great wickedness and the destruction of the people by the flood.

The great age of those who lived in this period may have been a provision of nature for the promotion of a rapid increase of the race and for the advancement of knowledge. The revelation of God to them could thereby be the better preserved. Then, too, the body of man was not originally subject to death and when it became so because of his sin, the process of decay may have been less rapid. And, besides, the effect of hereditary disease had not begun to effect and weaken the race.

The Great Wickedness. As indicated above, this Wickedness seemed to arise from the intermarriage of the descendants of Seth and those of Cain. The descendants of Seth were called "the song of God," because they were the religious seed. When they looked upon the beautiful daughters of Cain (called the daughters of man because they represented the irreligious portion of the race), they married them and thereby brought the whole race into such corruption that "every imagination of the thought of his heart was only evil continually" (Gen. 6:5). God therefore declared "My Spirit shall not always strive with man" and set the limit when he should quit thus striving with him at one-hundred and twenty years (Gen. 6:3). After that God proposed to destroy the whole wicked race from off the face of the earth (Gen. 6:7).

Noah God's Chosen Man. The narrative tells us (Gen. 6:8) that "Noah found favor in the eyes of Jehovah." This was no doubt because his character and acts were acceptable to Him. He was the tenth and last in the Sethic line. He was the son of Lamech (Gen. 5:28), a godly man, who had felt the weight of burden because of the curse which God had pronounced upon the ground because of Adam's sin. He was called Noah by his father, because he said the child would be a source of comfort concerning their toil growing out of that curse (Gen. 5:39). He was a just and perfect man and walked with God (Gen. 6:9; 7:1). Compare also I Peter 3:20 and Heb. 11:7. He is also called a preacher of righteousness (II Peter 2:5) and it is probable that, during the one-hundred and twenty years that were likely employed in building the ark, he preached to his generation and tried to lead them to repentance. He was, however, unable to influence any save his own family. The saving of his own family was, however, a splendid monument of his life.

The Ark. Noah built the ark according to the pattern given him by Jehovah. It was a sort of box-like boat 525 ft. long 87-1/2 ft. wide and 42-1/2 ft. deep, if we count a cubit at twenty-one inches. It was three stories high, and the building of it was a huge undertaking. We need not, however, think of it as an undertaking beyond the resources of the times. All those early people seem to have been fond of colossal works. The building of this Ark was not only an object lesson to the ungodly people of the time but a satisfactory proof of the faith of the builder.

The Flood. At the command of Jehovah Noah and his household entered the Ark carrying two of every species of unclean, and seven of every clean kind of animal and creeping things. They were shut in by the hand of God. The scripture passes silently over all horrors that filled the earth as man and beast were destroyed. We may imagine them trying by strength to get out of reach of the rising waters, but no mental culture or mechanical skill or physical culture, neither tears and entreaties could deliver man from the destruction which God had determined because of sin. It was seven months before the Ark rested on Ararat and more than five more before the ransomed company departed from it.

The Sacrifice and Rainbow Covenant. Upon leaving the Ark Noah expressed his thanksgiving and devotion to God by erecting an altar to Jehovah and offering thereon a sacrifice consisting of victims of every species of clean bird and beast. The fragrance of this sacrifice, such as the world had never seen before, was pleasant to Jehovah and he visited Noah with a promise that he would not again send such a flood upon the earth. The rainbow was given as a pledge of the promise made him. It was to be the constant seal of mercy on God's part, and it is not necessary to worry over the question as to whether there had never been a rainbow before or whether it was simply appropriated as a sign. In this new covenant the earth was put under Noah, as it was under Adam at first. He was, however, allowed to eat flesh, only mans blood was not to be shed and the seasons were to continue in regularity. Thus the race started anew as a saved group, rescued through the faith of Noah.

Confirmation of Tradition and Geology. Perhaps no other event of scripture history has found so large a place in ancient traditions and legends as has the flood. It is found in each of the three great races-the Semites; the Aryan; and the Tutarian. It is found alike among savage and civilized races, and as might be expected is most accurate in the countries that were nearest to where the Ark rested. Among the most important of these early traditions are those of Babylon. Greece, China, and America. In a general way these traditions may be said to agree with the Biblical story in the following particulars: (1) That a flood destroyed an evil world; (2) That one righteous family was saved in a boat and that animals were saved with them; (3) That the boat landed on a mountain; (4) That a bird was sent out of the boat; (5) That the saved family built an altar and worshiped God with sacrifice. All these stories tend to corroborate the Biblical story and to show that the whole race must have spring from this common home from which they have been scattered abroad.

Geology has also done much to confirm the flood story. Geologists are well acquainted with facts in world history that bring the flood "entirely within the range of natural phenomena." The Scripture (Gen. 7:11) speaks of the fountains of the deep being broken, language that could refer to the inrushing of the sea upon a depression of the earth which later rose again. Such elevations and depressions have occurred many times. An example is the elevation of the coast of Chile by an earthquake in 1822. Such an explanation by no means destroys the miracle of it, since the coming just when Noah had completed the ark and entered it and just when God said it would come, provided the element of miracle. A wide-spread flood is also required by the discovery of evidence in the earth of the destruction of animal life.

Some Teachings of This Period. The teachings of this period may be divided into three groups: Those concerning Cain and Abel; those concerning Cain and Seth. or the two races; those concerning the flood.

Those concerning Cain and Abel are: (1) The mere fact of having worshiped is not a guarantee of acceptance with God. (2) Both the spirit and the form of worship must please Jehovah. (3) God tries to point out the right way to men and only punishes when man fails to give heed. (4) Man is free and though God may turn to show him a better way, he will not restrain him by force even from the worst crimes. (5) To try to shun the responsibility of being our brother's keeper is to show the spirit of Cain.

The story of Cain and Seth, or the two races show: (1) That our acts reveal our thoughts. (2) That the indulgence of our lusts and appetites disgraces the noblest people. (3) That outward culture without true religion will not save a people. (4) The noble and good will finally dominate other men.

The story of the flood teaches: (1) That Jehovah can not make men righteous against their will. (2) That men by wickedness grieve God and thwart his purposes. (3) That man has, therefore, power to cause his own destruction. (4) That God does not save because of numbers or civilization, but because of character and obedience to his laws. (5) That God is pleased with the worship of those who obey him.

For Study and Discussion, (1) The consequences of sin as seen in this period with special reference to the new truths added to those of the former period. (2) New truths about God. (3) The beginning of the arts of civilization. (4) The unity of the race. (S) The names and ages of the six oldest men and whether any one of them could have known personally both Adam and Noah. (6) The size, architecture and the task of building the Ark. (7) The flood as a whole. (8) The inhabitants of the Ark. (9) The departure from the Ark, and the new covenant. (10) The flood as a divine judgment especially in the light of the judgment put upon Adam and Cain. (11) Noah as the first man mentioned who saved others and the way in which he represents Jesus. (12) Evidences of man's freedom as seen in this and the former chapters. (13) Worship as seen in the two periods studied.

CHAPTER III

From the Flood to Abraham.

Gen. Chs. 9-11.

Noah's Shame and Prophecy. Just what the vocation of Noah bad been before his call to prepare for the flood we do not know. But after the flood, perhaps compelled by necessity, he became an husbandman. He had probably settled on the slopes or in the valleys of Ararat where he planted a vineyard. On one occasion at least he fell under the intoxicating influence of the fermented wine. This man upon whom God had conferred such great favor and who alone preserved the race alive lay naked and helpless in his tent.

In this shameful condition he was discovered by his sons whose conduct led him in a spirit of prophecy to assign to his three sons the rewards and punishments which their deeds merited. The punishment and rewards fell upon the descendants of his sons. The descendants of Ham, because of his joy rather than sorrow over the sin and humiliation of his father, should always be a servile race. Out of these descendants of Ham arose the Canaanites, the Babylonians and the Egyptians who developed the three great civilizations of antiquity. Their ascendancy, however, soon passed. The Canaanites were subdued by the Israelites; the Cushites of Chaldea were absorbed by Semitic conquerors and Carthage of the Phoenicians fell before her foes. The sons of Cush, in the scripture commonly meaning the Ethiopian and now known as the black-skinned African, are the very synonym for weakness, degradation and servitude.

The descendants of Japheth and Shem like those of Ham can be traced only in part. The Japhethites probably settled around the Mediterranean and in the northwest beyond the Black Sea. From them "the great races of Europe, including the Greeks, the Romans, and the more modern nations, must have sprung." The Shemites were located, generally speaking, between the territories occupied by the sons of Ham and Japheth. Aram, one of the sons of Japheth, settled in Syria

10

near Damascus in northern part of Mesopotamia and through his son, Uz, gave the name of Uz to the territory, thus showing how that branch of the Hebrews came from western Mesopotamia, a fact now confirmed by modern discovery. All the other sons of Shem and their descendants are dropped from the record of Chapter eleven, except that of Arphaxad from whom descended Abram.

The prophecy of Noah was not only fulfilled in the case of Ham and his punishment but in the blessing of the Others. Shem was for a long time signally blessed as is witnessed by the Asiatic supremacy and especially in the Jews who conquered the Canaanites (descendants of Ham) and in whose tents God dwelt. During that period of the ascendancy of the Shemites not much was known of the descendants of Japheth. But now for more than two thousand years his have been the dominant race of the earth. Year by year, the Japhethites have spread over the globe, until whole continents are now peopled by him. He now rests his foot upon every soil either as a trader, colonist or national power.

The Tower of Babel. The place of this tower is in the land of Shinat, which is the name given by the early Hebrews to the land of Babylonia (Gen. 10:10; 14:19; Is. 11:1; Dan. 1:2; Zech. 5:11). This plain of Shinar had become the center of the earth's population. They threw up with infinite toil great mounds, which still stand as monuments of human achievement. Many such mounds and ruins, any of which would have seemed lofty in contrast with the level plain of Babylon, may be seen by the traveler.

The exact location of this tower cannot be determined with certainty, but it has been thought by some that a great mound on the east of the Euphrates, which probably represents the remains of the great temple of Marduk with its huge pyramid-like foundation, was the site of this tower. On the west of the Euphrates, however, is a vast mound called Birs Nimrood, which used to be regarded as the ruins of the Tower of Babel. The fact that it early gave the impression of incompleteness favors this claim. Nebuchadnezzar says on a tablet that another king began it but left it unfinished. It fell into disrepair and was completed by Nebuchadnezzar and was used as one of the great temples. It was built of brick and was oblong in form. It measured seven hundred yards around and rose to a height of from one hundred and fifty to two hundred feet high. It consisted o? seven stages or stories colored to represent the tints which the Sabeans thought appropriate to the seven planets. Beginning from the bottom they were black, orange, bright red, golden, pale yellow, dark blue and silver, representing respectively the colors of Saturn, Jupiter, Mars, the Sun, Venus. Mercury, and the Moon. These marks may indicate the prevalence of idolatry and have led some to think the tower of Babel was intended to do honor to the gods of Babylonia.

The specific purpose of this tower is difficult to determine. Josephus says the object was to save the people in case of another flood. The scripture record (11:4) indicates that they were moved by an unholy pride and selfish desire to make for themselves a great name. It also was intended to become a sort of rallying-point which would keep the people together and prevent the destruction of their glory which they thought would result from their separation. In 11:6 God says "nothing will be restrained from them which they have imagined to do." In this there is an implication that they are at cross purposes with God. It was an act that defied God and showed the need of punishment. It is not unlikely that idolatry had begun to prevail and that the tower was built in honor of those false Gods whom men were disposed to trust.

The incompleteness of the tower is attributed to divine intervention. Hitherto all the descendants of Noah had spoken the same language, but now by a direct divine interposition they are caused to speak several, and then separated so they can no longer cooperate with each other in carrying out their plans which had so displeased God. The different languages then are regarded as a punishment of the race which had rebelled against God.

Traditions of such a tower may be found in many forms and in many countries. In Babylonia there was a tradition that not long after the flood men were tall and strong and became so puffed up that they defied the gods and tried to erect a tower called Babylon by means of which they could scale heaven. But when it reached the sky the gods sent a mighty wind and turned over the tower. They said that hitherto all men had used the same language, but that at this time there was sent on them a confusion of many tongues, from which confusion the tower was named Babel. In Greece, there was a legend in which we trace the story of the tower of Babel. According to this legend a race of giants

12

tried to reach Mount Olympus, which was supposed to be the residence of the gods, by piling Mount Ossa upon Pelion. But the gods interfered with their plan and scattered the impious conspirators. This effort of the Titans to mount up to heaven corresponds so well to the motive of the builders of the tower as to indicate that there was a common origin for both stories.

There is also a Greek tradition that Helen had three sons: Aeolus, Dorus, and Ion, who were the ancestors of the three great branches of the Hellenic race. This again corresponds to the prophetic table of nations which were to descend from Shem, Ham, and Japheth, the three sons of Noah.

The Civilization of the Ancient World. Just when and where civilization began we have no means of telling. The Bible speaks of a very high state of civilization at a very early time (Gen. 4:20-22). In ages long before Abraham and Moses the world had made great advancement in culture, commerce, law and religion. From the monuments and engraven vases that have been found in such unearthed cities as Nippur, we now know that Abraham and Moses did not live in a crude and undeveloped age, but, as the Bible would imply, in an age of great progress. We even learn that long before their time there was a most complete and complex civilization.

Two Great Empires of Antiquity. It is impossible to tell which of two great nations, the Chaldeans and the Egyptians, first attained to a high state of civilization. They appear to have started very early in the race, the Chaldeans in the plains on the banks of the Euphrates and the Egyptians in the plains on the banks of the Nile. They seem to have made about equal progress in all the arts of civilization.

Nimrod, a descendent of Ham, is declared to be the founder of the Chaldean Empire. His exploits as a hunter seem to have aided him to the throne. He began to reign at Babel and had a number of cities in the plain of Shinar. Later he went out in the district of Assyria and built Ninevah and a number of other cities. From the Assyrian and Chaldean ascriptions, we have learned much of the Accadians, whose influence carried forward that early civilization. We thereby confirm the Biblical claim that it was under Nimrod the Cushite, and not through the Semitic race, that the Chaldean kingdom began.

Of the beginning of the Egyptian empire, the other great center of civilization, we have no certain knowledge. So far as the records of the scriptures or of the earliest records to which the monuments bear witness, Egypt comes before us full grown. The further back we go the more perfect and developed do we find the organization of the country. The activity and industry of the Egyptians, their power of erecting great buildings and of executing other laborious tasks at this early period is a marvel to all ages. It has been shown by Prof. Petrie that some of the blocks in at least one of the great pyramids were cut by tubular drills fitted with diamond points or something similar. This to us is a very modern invention.

At least thirty dynasties of kings (according to Manetho) ruled Egypt in succession. At least twelve of these must have reigned in Egypt before Jacob and his sons settled within their borders. Many of the great monuments and some of the largest of the pyramids were already to be seen before Abraham visited that country. There had been constant progress in all kinds of learning and art, and a highly advanced society and government had been attained when the Bible history first came in contact with it.

Commerce was carried on extensively on both land and sea. Long before the time of Moses a stream of caravans were on the road between Egypt and Babylon, passing through Canaan. Treaties were made between different states whereby these caravans were protected and given safe passage through the countries traversed. Three thousand years before Christ the Phoenicians sent out ships from Tyre that had intercourse with the cities of the Mediterranean and later with England and sailed around Africa and traded on the Red Sea and the Persian Gulf. Egypt sent sea expeditions to South Africa in the sixteenth century before Christ. All of this suggests how much more of geography these ancients knew than we are accustomed to think.

Language and Literature. It is impossible to say what was the original language. But that men once spoke the same language and that the varieties of human tongues arose from some remarkable cause is in some degree confirmed by the research of modern scholarship. The Bible alone states clearly what that cause was. All existing languages belong to three great families: the Aryan, the Semitic, and the Turanian. These correspond roughly to three sons of Noah: Shem, Ham and Japheth.

14

In the time of Abraham and long before, and on to the time of Moses there was great literary culture. Letters passed between kingdoms and cities. There were schools and colleges, great dictionaries and many books on many subjects. The Babylonian language was almost universally employed, so that the scribes could read without difficulty a letter sent anywhere in Egypt, Babylon, Canaan, or Arabia. This unity makes the translation of inscriptions on the monuments comparatively easy.

We know nothing of the origin of writing. As far back as we go into their history we find, already developed, a most complex system of writing and large libraries both in the royal cities and in small towns.

The Motive of Their Civilization. This is not difficult to find. The old Babylonian kings were called Priest Kings, and built their empires, temples, and cities, and exhibited such wonderful activities from a religious motive. The great mounds on the plain of Shinar, and the pyramids of Egypt are the eternal monuments of the religious devotion of these ancient people. Their religion was, however, filled with all sorts of idolatrous abuses and God called Abraham to be the leader of a purer religious life and to be the father of a people from whom would come the Great Revealer of all religious truth.

The Lessons of this Period. The stories of this period have for us several valuable lessons, among which the following are most vital. (I) All races had a common origin and are, therefore, vitally related. (2) By tracing the origin of the different races, we are shown Israel's place in the family of nations. (3) Since all nations are but branches of the same great family, all men are brothers. (4) The Hebrews are deeply interested in all of their neighbors, and their unique history can only be understood, in their true relation, as a part of the ancient Semitic world. (5) God exercises a common rule over all nations. (6) Civilization at this early age had reached a great advancement. (7) Men had reached a stage of great wickedness and because of their defiance of God were punished both by the confusion of tongues and by being scattered far and wide.

For Study and Discussion. (1) The genealogies of Noah's sons. (2) The different places where his descendants settled, the cities they built and the names of those connected with each. Study the geography. (3) Through which of Noah's sons the Messiah came and through which of his sons. (4) Lessons from the shame of Noah and the spirit of his sons.

(5) The nature and fulfillment of his prophecies concerning his sons. (6) The universality of the race and the origin of the nations. (7) The teachings of the tower of Babel. (8) The origin of different languages and the relation of languages to the creation of separate nations. (9) The traditions of other peoples and their relation and correspondence to the stories of this section. (10) The evidence of ancient monuments that corroborate or throw light upon the meaning of this section of the scripture. (11) The civilization of that early time compared with that of our time.

CHAPTER IV

From Abraham to Egypt..

Gen. Chs. 12-50.

The Events of the Period. The events of this period may be put down somewhat as follows: (1) Abraham's call and settlement in Canaan, chs. 12-13. (2) The rescue of Lot from the plundering kings of the North, ch. 14. (3) God makes a covenant with Abraham, ch. 15. (4) The birth and disposal of Ishmael, ch. 16. (5) The Promise of Isaac, ch. 17. (8) The destruction of Sodom and Gomorrah, chs. 18-19. (7) Abraham lives at Gerar. Isaac is born and sacrificed, chs. 20-22. (8) Sarah's death, ch. 23. (9) Isaac is married, ch. 24. (10) Abraham and Ishmael die and Isaac's two sons, ch. 25. (11) Isaac dwells in Gerar and Jacob steals his brother's birthright, chs. 26-27. (12) Jacob's experiences as a fugitive and his roll and settlement in Canaan, chs. 28-36. Joseph's career and the settlement of the nation in Egypt, chs. 37-50.

The Purpose of Narrative. In this section we have given us, in brief form, the career of Abraham, Isaac and Jacob and their families and how we received the promises through them. Ages have passed since Noah and the people had grown wicked and turned from Jehovah to other gods. God had promised not to destroy the world with another flood, but he must employ other and new means. He, therefore, selects a man and in him a nation that should be his representative on earth. With this man and nation God would deposit his truth and in it the hopes of the race until the time when Christ the redeemer should come.

We pass, therefore, from the consideration of the beginnings of the history of the race and from the general history to the story of one man, Abraham and the chosen family and nation. All the rest of the Old Testament is an account of the victories and defeats of this nation.

The Conditions of the Times. At the time of Abraham three countries are of special interest, Chaldea, Egypt and Canaan. Outwardly there was a splendid civilization as is shown by the monuments. There

17

were great cities with splendid palaces, temples and libraries. "There were workers in fabrics, metals, stones, implements and ornaments." Time was divided as now and sun-dials showed the time of day. Great systems of canals existed and the country was in a high state of cultivation. The pyramids were already old and a great stone wall had long ago been built across the isthmus of Suez to prevent the immigrants and enemies of the north from coming down upon them. In Tyre and Sidon there were great glass works and dying factories. There were also vast harbors crowded with sea going ships. Luxurious living was to be found everywhere.

Inwardly, however, there was a corrupt moral condition, which was hastening the nations to decay and to a ruin such as amazes all the world to this day. Ur of the Chaldees, the birth place and home of Abraham, was the seat of the great temple of the moon-god, and this sanctuary became so famous that the moon-god was known throughout all northern Syria as the Baal or Lord of Haran. The bad state of the times is suggested by Sodom and Gomorrah and their fate. For these cities were perhaps only typical of the entire civilization of the time.

In such a time and out of such a civilization God called Abraham, who should found a new nation that would serve him and form the basis of a new civilization. He also selected Canaan as the home of this new people. It was the geographical center of all the ancient world and a revelation of God made there would soon be know among all nations.

The Confirmations of the Biblical Record. Each new excavation made in the ruins of the ancient, long-buried, cities throws new light upon the scriptures and always confirms its statements. There are on the tablets of clay found in the old libraries statements concerning the social, commercial, religious and political conditions of the time of Abraham and before and all of them agree with the statements of Genesis. There has been found a record of the years of famine and the Pharaohs of the time have been determined.

The kings who captured Lot are now known. The Bible has suffered nothing at all from the knowledge gained from the ancient records.

The Experiences of Abraham. The call of Abraham as recorded In this section is probably from Ur of the Chaldees to Haran where his father died (11:31-32). His call is the most important event in the history of God's kingdom since the fall of man. It was indeed a new starting point for that kingdom. The call was accompanied by a promise or covenant in which God bound himself not to withdraw from Abraham (15:17-21). The call and work, together with the promises, may be put down somewhat as follows:

1. It was a call to separation from his home and native land. He was a large shepherd-farmer with large flocks and herds and a number of slaves. The family was perhaps of high rank in his country and there was a warm family affection in his family. Many others had gone from his country to the regions of the Mediterranean but always for gain or selfish betterment, Abraham went in obedience to the divine call. There was no selfishness in his move. He went for conscience' sake, somewhat as the Pilgrims, forsaking all the ties of nature that bound them to England, sailed to America in the Mayflower.

2. It was a call to service. The people of his time were falling into idolatry. Even Terah, his father, was an idolater and reputed to have been a maker of idol images. He was to serve the one true God and to stand for principle where everyone was against him. He was to enter into covenant relations with God and stand alone with him where all social and national customs were hostile.

3. It was a call to found a nation. The promise was to make of him a great nation that should have as its main purpose the service of the one God. God foresaw the ruin that was to come to all the nations of Abraham's time and prepared him and in him a new and spiritual nation which would produce a new and godly civilization. He died when Jacob was but a lad and did not see the fulfillment of the promise of the nation that should outlast Egypt or Babylon.

4. It was a call to be the father of a son. In 17:16 God promised him a son, Isaac, in whom his seed should be called (21:12). Out of him was to come a blessing to all nations. This promise was fulfilled in Christ, through whom all the nations of the earth have been blessed. Just as in Isaac Abraham became the head of a great earthly seed that should be as the sand of the sea, so in Jesus he should be the head of a great spiritual seed that should be as the stars of the heaven for numbers.

God often repeats his covenant and promises with Abraham, Gen. 12:1-7; 13:14-17; 15:1-21; 17:1-8; 18:18; 22:16-18. He often renews it in the generations to come as to Isaac, Gen. 26:1-5, and to Jacob, Gen. 28:10-15.

19

The Character of Abraham. How great is the name of Abraham today! He is revered by Jews, Mohammedans and Christians (ch. 12:2). In all history there is not a nobler character. The story of his life shows him to have been shrewd in business, of good temper, of warm domestic affections and possessed of much calm wisdom. He was generous in his dealings with others, looking well after their interests. He often made sacrifices for the well-being of others. The most significant thing about him, however, was his attitude toward God. His chief desire was to obey God. Wherever he went he erected an altar to God and in everything he manifested reverence, confidence, love and submission toward God. This is the chief element of his greatness.

The Character and Career of Isaac. The life of Isaac has but little in it that is of special interest. He probably spent most of his life in a quiet home near, or in Hebron. This has been taken to suggest that he was of a quiet and retiring disposition. He was not a man of energy and force of character such as Abraham, his father, but he had all his father's reverence for God. His faith in God was rewarded with a renewal of the promises which Abraham had received.

Among the incidents of his life that should be noted are the following: (1) His experience on Mount Moriah, when his father in obedience to God prepared to sacrifice him in worship. Such sacrifice was common in Babylonia, Phoenicia and Canaan. The submission to his father's will and evident obedience to the divine will indicated would seem to point to his faith in God. While he does not mention the matter himself and it is not referred to again in this section, the experience must have had much influence on his whole career. (2) The second notable event of his life was his marriage. In this story there is preserved the ancient customs of his father's provision for the marriage of the son. The story also shows the overruling influence of deity in his marriage. The whole experience was calculated to show his sincere relation to God who was leading. (3) The birth of his twin sons Esau and Jacob. They were so different in type that their descendants for centuries showed a like difference and even became antagonistic. Jacob was ambitious and persevering. Esau was frank and generous but shallow and unappreciative of the best things. The birthright carried with it two advantages: (1) The headship of the family. (2) A double portion of the inheritance (Dt. 21:15-17). Jacob set great value upon it,

20

while Esau preferred a good dinner. Isaac's latter days were made dark because of the relation of these sons.

Stories Concerning Jacob. These are calculated to show that Jacob was clever and far-sighted and was willing to employ any mean, honorable or dishonorable, to gratify his ambition. They also show his suffering for his unfair acts and his final change to a new man. His deception of his father resulted in his becoming a fugitive from home and never again seeing his mother who aided him in his treachery. He was treated by Laban just as he himself had treated his brother. For twenty years he was deprived of the quiet and friendly life of his old home.

While away he had some religious experiences that made him a new man. His vision at Bethel taught him that Jehovah his God was also caring for him though in a strange land. He may have thought that Jehovah dwelt only among the people of his nation and that on leaving home he was also going beyond the protection of God. As a result he erected here a sanctuary that became sacred to all the Hebrews.

His struggle at the brook Jabbok made Jacob a new man. He had all along depended on his own wits. Now he is ready to return to his brother and show sorrow for his conduct. The incident is parallel to the struggle which a repentant man must wage against his lower nature. When the struggle is over he is a new man, a prince of god. Religion had become real to him and his whole future career is built on a new plan. He is still inventive and ambitious and persevering but is God's man doing God's will.

In connection with Jacob we have also the lessons concerning Esau. He was a man intent upon immediate physical enjoyment; an idle drifter without spiritual ideals. From his character and that of the Edomites, his descendants, there is taught the lesson that such an unambitious man or nation will always become degenerate and prove a failure. God himself cannot make a man out of an idle drifter.

The Stories About Joseph. The moral value of these stories is very great. They are told in a charm that is felt by all. The literary power and unity is remarkable. There is seen in them ideals of integrity and truthfulness. He is cheerful and uncomplaining and no adversity could destroy his ambitions. The study of this section will well reward a frequent review of it.

21

All the materials may be grouped around the following principal great periods or incidents of his life. (1) His childhood, where we find him petted and spoiled but ambitious and trustworthy and hated by his brethren. (2) His sale to the Egyptians and separation from his house and kindred, this including his slavery and the faithfulness he showed in such a position. (3) His position as overseer and his loyalty together with his temptation and unjust imprisonment. (4) His exaltation to the governorship of Egypt with his provisions for the famine and change of the whole system of land tenure, which put it all under royal control. It would also include his kindness to his father's family in providing for their preservation.

The stories have in them several elements that need to be noticed. (1) There are many sudden and striking contrasts. Such are his changes from a petted and spoiled boy in the home to a slave in Egypt; from an overseer of his master's house to a prisoner in the dungeon; for that dungeon to the governor of the powerful empire of the age. (2) His success is never based on or promoted by a miracle but is assured because he is of value to others. He wins no promotions by means of armor or conquests of power but by faithfulness to those whom he served. His is a conquest made by business sagacity. He is a hero of usefulness. (3) The use of his position to advance the interests of others is altogether out of line with the views of western students of society. We would hardly think it right for one to so earnestly promote the interests of a heathen sovereign as Joseph did in the case of his slave master and of Pharaoh. (4) The pathos and depth of feeling is not surpassed in all literature. This is especially true in the story of his relations with his brethren when they visit Egypt. Pent up emotion tugs at one's heart as one reads of the anxiety of the brothers, the fear of the fear of the father, and the burning affection of Joseph. The spirit of forgiveness and love for his humble kinsmen fill one with admiration.

The death of Jacob and Joseph. Jacob was greatly prospered and died at a ripe old age. He asked to be buried in Canaan and Joseph after having him embalmed went, accompanied by his kindred and friends, to Canaan and buried him according to his request. Before his death, he pronounced upon his sons a blessing that promised great increase in numbers and in political power.

After the death of Jacob, Joseph continued to show kindness to his brethren. Before his death, at the age of one hundred and ten years, he prophesied that God would come and lead them out of Egypt and took an oath of them that they would carry up his bones to the land of Canaan into which they would be delivered.

In Jacob's blessing on his sons and in Joseph's prophecy of their removal by God and his promises, they saw the providence of God in all the future of the race and expected its triumph.

These stories typical. The stories of this section are commonly thought to be typical of New Testament truth. While it is probably not best to make too much of this typical idea, it is safe to say that much of it is illustrative of such New Testament teachings. The career of Abraham, Isaac and Joseph each at some point or points suggests the life and work of Jesus. Abraham is called or appointed of God to be the head of a spiritual nation, he has revealed to him the will of God, he intercedes for a wicked Sodom and saved lot, all of which suggests the attitude and work of Jesus. Isaac is an only son, is offered in sacrifice, has secured for him a bride in a most unusual manner. This again in many ways illustrates the attitude and work of the Savior. But Joseph is perhaps more highly figurative of the Redeemer. His being hated and cast out by his brethren is like the rejection of Jesus; the way his wicked brethren came to him in their extremity and received forgiveness and sustenance suggest how a sinner finds mercy and life in Jesus; his prosperity and honor gained among others and the final coming of his brethren to him is suggestive in many of the details of the way the Jews rejected Jesus and of how, after Jesus has gained great power among Gentile nations, the Jews will finally repent of their national sin and accept the crucified Savior as the Jews' Messiah; the whole story of the humiliation, sufferings and exaltation of Joseph correspond to like events in the career of Jesus.

Social and Religious Conditions of the Times. There is little to suggest anything savage or barbarous. The spirit and language of courtesy is everywhere present. There is great hospitality and the marriage relation was respected by such heathen rulers as Pharaoh and Abimelech. When property was bought and sold the contracts were formal and were held sacred even though the owner was long absent as in the case of Abraham who bought the cave of Machpelah. Rebekah had bracelets, ear-rings, jewels of silver and of gold, and fine raiment as elements of adornment. There were slaves but they were kindly treated and made almost as part of the family. Wealthy people as Jacob employed their sons in the ordinary occupations such as caring for the sheep. In Egypt and Chaldea the arts were highly developed and there was much learning.

The worship of the patriarchs was very simple. They erected simple altars and offered on them burnt offerings. The erection of such altars and making such open profession of their worship were always among their first acts when they settled in a new place. There are some evidences that they observed the Sabbath of rest. Abraham gave a tithe to Melchizedek and Jacob promised God to do the same if he would bless him. God communed with them and gave them knowledge of his will and especially promised them great future blessing, through a deliverer that would come through the line of Abraham, Isaac, Jacob and Judah.

The Book of Job. There has been a general belief that the incidents recorded in the book of Job belong to this period or even to an earlier time. There is no mention of the bondage in Egypt nor of any of the early Hebrew patriarchs. The Sabeans and Chaldeans were Job's neighbor! and he lived "in the east" where the first settlements of mankind were made. The social religious and family life as portrayed in this book correspond to those of this period. There was art and invention; there was understanding of astronomy and mining; there was a fine family affection and evidences of social kindness and benevolence; there was high development of commerce and government; there was both the true and false or idolatrous worship. This book should be read following the outline given in the author's The Bible Book by Book.

Lessons of the Period. It would be difficult to point out all the splendid lessons brought forward by these narratives but the following are among the more important ones. (1) God guides to a noble destiny all those who will be guided by him. (2) God reveals himself to all those who seek a revelation, no matter in what place or land, if only they are in the path of duty, (3) Unselfish service always brings a blessed reward. (4) God's blessing and guidance are not confined to Israel but are extended to other nations also. (5) A noble ambition, courage, unselfishness and childlike faith in God's leadership make men valuable to others in every age and walk of life. (6) A man or nation without spiritual ideal and bent on physical enjoyment will soon become degenerate as did Esau. (7) Even a fugitive, fleeing from his own crimes, is followed by the divine love and in his saddest moments and amidst his most discouraging surrounding circumstances is given glorious revelations. (8) In the divine providence our misfortunes of life often develop our nobler impulses of heart. (9) Unjust adversity cannot destroy a man of faith and integrity of character, if only he manifest a cheerful and helpful spirit. (10) God overrules evil for good, so that all things can bring good to them that love God. (11) Loyalty to unfortunate kindred in the time of success is a sure sign of nobility of character.

For Study and Discussion. (1) The several appearances of God to Abraham: (a) The purpose of each; (b) its influence in the life of Abraham. (2) The promises made to Abraham and renewed to Isaac and Jacob noting the progressive nature of the revelation seen in these promises. (3) Select four prominent persons besides Abraham, Isaac, Jacob, and Joseph, sketched in the section, and study them. (4) The other nations introduced in the narrative. (5) The moral condition of the times. (6) The worship of God seen in the section. (7) The points of weakness and strength in each of the patriarchs mentioned. (8) The disappointments and family troubles of Jacob as seen in the light of his early deceptions. (9) Other illustrations that a man will reap whatever he sows. (10) The strong family ties, seen especially in the matter of marriage. (11) The fundamental value of faith in life. (12) God's judgment and blessings of heathen people on behalf of his own chosen people. (13) The different immigrations of Abraham and others. (14) The places of historical importance mentioned. (15) The promises or types and symbols of Christ and the New Testament times.

CHAPTER V

From Egypt to Sinai.

Ex Chs. 1-19.

Israel in Egypt. The length of time the Hebrews remained In Egypt is a perplexing question. Exodus 6:16-20 makes Moses the fourth generation from Levi (See Gen. 15:16; Num. 26:57-59). This would make it about 150 years. Gen. 15:13 predicts 400 years. Ex. 12:40 says they were there 430 years and Paul (Gal. 3:17) says 430 years from Abraham to Sinai. These apparently conflicting dates may be explained because of different methods of counting generations, probably based on long lives of men of that period or they may have had a different point to mark the beginning and end of the sojourn. If the Pharaoh of Joseph was one of the Hyksos or Shepherd kings, as has been the common view, and if the Pharaoh "that knew not Joseph" was, as is the general belief, Rameses II, the period of 430 years would about correspond to the historical data.

Their oppression grew out of the fear of the king lest they should assist some of the invaders that constantly harassed Egypt on the North. They may have assisted the shepherd kings under whom Joseph has risen and who had just been expelled. To cripple and crush them there was given them hard and exhaustive tasks of brick making under cruel task-masters. There still remains evidence of this cruelty in the many Egyptian buildings built of brick, made of mud mixed with straw and dried in the sun. When it was found that they still increased in number in spite of the suffering. Pharoah tried, at first privately then publicly, to destroy all the male children. This order does not seem to have been long in force but was a terrible blow to a people like the Hebrews whose passion for children, and especially for male children, has always been proverbial.

It is difficult to gather from this narrative the varied influence of this sojourn upon the Hebrews themselves. They doubtless gained much of value from the study of the methods of warfare and military equipment of the Egyptians. They learned much of the art of agriculture and from the social and political systems of this enlightened people. No doubt many of their choicest men received educational training that fitted them for future leadership. Their suffering seems on the one hand to have somewhat deadened them, destroying ambition. On the other, it bound them together by a common bond and prepared the way for the work of Moses, the deliverer, and for the real birth of the nations.

Moses the Deliverer. Chapters 2 and 4 tell the wonderful story of the birth of Moses, of his loyalty to his people, of his sojourn in Midian and of his final call to the task of the deliverance of Israel. His wonderful life-a life to which all the centuries are indebted-is naturally divided into three parts. (1) His early life of forty years at the court of Pharaoh. By faith his parents trusted him to the care of Providence and he was brought to the house of Pharoah and was taught in all the learning of the Egyptians, who conducted great universities and were highly cultured in the arts and sciences (Acts 7:22). Finally feeling it to be his duty to renounce his worldly glory and identify himself with his Hebrew brethren, he made the choice by faith (Heb. 11:24-27). He no doubt felt then the call to be their deliverer but did not find his countrymen ready to accept him as such (Acts 7:25-28). Whereupon he fled to the wilderness of Midian. (2) Forty years in the desert where he gained an intimate knowledge of all the wilderness through which for forty years he was to lead the Hebrews in their wanderings. Here he had opportunity to learn patience and meditate and gain the ability to wait on God. Here God finally appeared to him and gave him definite and ample instructions for his task of delivering out of bondage this crushed and ignorant slave race and for making of them a nation of the purest spiritual and moral ideals the world has ever known. (3) Forty years as leader and lawgiver for Israel while they tabernacled in the wilderness.

Perhaps three reasons led Moses to undertake the task of leaving Midian and championing the cause of Israel. (1) He had a vision of God the holy one of all power who would be with him. (2) The conviction that the time was ripe, because of the death of the king of Egypt and the years of weak government that followed. (3) By over-ruling all objections God gave him an overwhelming sense of his responsibility in the matter. He saw it as his personal duty.

The call of Moses consists of two elements. (1) The human element which consisted of a knowledge of the needs of the Hebrew people. To him, as to all great leaders and benefactors of the race, the cry of the oppressed or needy constituted the first element of a call to enlist in their service. (2) The divine element. God heard the cry of his people and remembered his covenant with Abraham and appeared to Moses in a burning bush and sent him to deliver them from under the tyranny of Pharaoh. Like Isaiah (Is. Ch.6) he not only saw the need of his people but also the holy God calling him to supply the need.

Moses task was three fold: (1) Religious: He was to show in Egypt weakness of the idolatrous worship and to establish in the wilderness the true worship of one and only God who is ruler of all. (2) Political: He was to overcome the power of the mighty Pharaoh and deliver a people of 600,000 men besides the children with their herds and flocks out of his territory. Then, too, he was to give them laws and so connect them together that as a nation they would survive the hostile nations around them and the civil strife and dissensions within. (3) Social: He was also called upon to provide rules by which, to keep clean not only the individual, but his family, and to teach them right relations to each other. In carrying out this program, it devolved upon him to provide an elaborate code of civil, sanitary, ceremonial, moral and religious laws.

The Great Deliverance. The deliverance may be properly considered in three sections. (1) The preparation. (2) The contest with Pharoah and the ten plagues. (3) The crossing of the Red Sea.

The preparation consists (1) in getting the people acquainted with what God intended to do and thereby secure their full consent to enter into the plan. Then, too, it was necessary to have a very thorough organization so that the expedition could proceed in an orderly way. (2) There were various preliminary appeals to Pharaoh with the consequent added burdens laid upon the Hebrews.

The contest with Pharaoh consisted of certain preliminary demands followed by ten national calamities intended to force the king to let the people go. The struggle was all based upon the request of Moses that all Israel be allowed to go three days' journey into the wilderness to serve their God. This gave the conflict a religious aspect and showed that the struggle was not merely one between Moses and Pharaoh, but between the God of Israel and the gods of Egypt.

28

All the plagues, therefore, had a distinct religious significance: (1) To show them the power of Jehovah (Ex. 7:17); (2) to execute judgment against the gods of Egypt (Ex. 12:12). Every plague was calculated to frustrate Egyptian worship or humiliate some Egyptian god. For example, the lice covered everything and were miserably polluting. All Egyptian worship was compelled to cease, since none of the priests could perform their religious service so long as any such insect had touched them since they went through a process of purification. In smiting the cattle with murrain, the sacred bull of Memphis was humiliated whether stricken himself or because of his inability to protect the rest of the cattle.

These plagues grew more severe with each new one. And much effort has been made to show that one would have led to another. Much has been said also, to show that the plagues, at least most of them, were events that were common in Egypt and that they were remarkable only for their severity. Such attempts to explain away the miraculous element are based upon the wrong view of a miracle. The very occurrence in response to the word of Moses and at such time as to each time meet a particular condition, or to make a certain desired impression, would put them out of the pale of the pale of the ordinary and into the list of the extraordinary or miraculous. At all events the sacred writer, the Hebrews in Egypt at the time, and the Egyptians all believed the strong hand of Jehovah was laid bare on behalf of his people. So it must seem to all who now believe that God rules in his universe.

In connection with and just preceding the tenth plague, there was instituted the Passover to celebrate their deliverance from Egypt and especially the passing of the Hebrew homes by the angel who went abroad in Egypt to slay the first born. It was this plaque that finally showed Pharaoh and his people the folly of resisting Jehovah and assured Israel of his power. The paschal lamb, whose blood sprinkled upon the door posts and lintels of the dwelling saved the Hebrew, is a beautiful type of Christ and his saving blood. This feast became one of great joy, annually celebrated, during all future Hebrew history.

The Crossing of the Red Sea. For three days and nights God led them by a pillar of cloud by day and of fire by night. At the end of the third day they had reached the shore of the Red Sea and were shut in by mountains on each side. They were greatly frightened to find that Pharaoh with a host of chariot-warriors was in close pursuit of them. But God caused the cloud that had been leading them to remove to their rear and to throw a shadow upon their enemies while giving power to the east wind (Ex. 14:21) that caused the waters of the sea to divide so they could cross on dry ground. When Pharaoh and his hosts attempted to follow then. God caused the waters to return and overwhelm them. As in former miracles, Moses was God's instrument in performing this miracle. When they were safe across and saw the overthrow of their enemies their feelings of joy expressed themselves in a great song of victory in which they ascribe praise to God and recount the incidents of his work of deliverance.

The Journey to Sinai. It is not possible to locate all the stations at which they stopped on their journey from the Red Sea to the time of their encampment at the foot of Horeb or Sinai. The list is given in Numbers, Chapter thirty-three. For our purpose it is sufficient to notice only a few places and incidents of the journey. (1) They encamped at Marah, being the first watering place they had found. The water, however, was bitter and could not be used until God had enabled Moses by a miracle to sweeten it. This was the first example of divine support for them. (2) At Elim they found water and shade and here God gave them the manna from heaven and the quail at eventide. Thus again Jehovah demonstrated his purpose to provide for their needs while wandering through the wilderness. This food was supplied to them continuously until they reached Canaan forty years later. (3) Under the leadership of the cloud, which during all the forty years of wilderness wandering, was their guide, they next encamped at Rephidim where there was no water at all. Here Moses by the command of God smote a rock and caused them to drink of a fountain thus opened for them. This rock is a suggestive type of Christ.

It was here also that they encountered and defeated the Amalekites, a tribe of Edomites, who still kept up the enmity of Esau their father against Jacob. Here also Jethro, Moses' father-in-law came to them bringing Moses wife and sons. Upon Jethro's advice the people were thoroughly organized. From Rephidim they came to Mount Sinai where they encamped for a whole year.

Lessons of the Period. The lessons of this period might be divided

30

into two classes. (1) Those of special value to the Hebrews themselves and lessons needed just then. (2) Those valuable for all time and all people. Among those of the first class, the following are worthy of record: (1) The authority of Moses was confirmed and the people were made ready for his teachings and leadership. (2) They were established in the popular belief in the goodness and power of Jehovah their God. Of the second and more general lessons, the following are highly important: (1) There is no chance in God's universe, but even the apparently unimportant events serve his purposes. (2) No human power whether of king or peasant or of nation can prevent the accomplishment of God's purposes. (3) Those who resist his power are overthrown as were the Egyptians, and those who act according to the divine will are elevated just as were the Israelites. (4) It is dangerous to oppose or harm God's people. He will avenge them. (5) Ample provisions are assured to those who will submit to divine leadership.

For Study and discussion. (1) The number of Hebrews that entered Egypt with Jacob, and the number that made the Exodus with Moses. (2) The Biblical story of their suffering while there, including the added burdens when Moses requested that they be allowed to go out to Egypt. (3) The birth, preservation and education of Moses. (4) Moses' forty years of wilderness training, its advantages and dangers. (5) The divine and human elements in Moses' call to be the deliverer. (6) The plagues, (a) the description of each, (b) the appropriateness and religious significance of each, (c) those imitated by Egyptian magicians, (d) those in which the Egyptians suffered and Israel did not. (7) The stubbornness of Pharaoh and his attempted compromises. (8) The miracles of this period other than the plagues. (9) God's provision and care for his people. (10) The murmurings of Israel. (11) The religious conditions of the times. (12) The geography of the country.

Chapter VI

From Sinai to Kadesh.

Ex. 20-Num. 14.

Mount Sinai. There are differences of opinion concerning the location of this mountain. It is sometimes called Horeb (Ex. 3:1; 17:6. etc.). All the Old Testament references to it clearly indicate that it was in the vicinity of Edom and connect it with Mt. Seir (Deut. 33:3; Judg. 5:4-5). Several points have been put forward as the probable site, but there can not now be any certainty as to the exact location. All the evidence both of the scripture and of the discoveries of archaeologists seem to point to one of the southwestern spurs of Mt. Seir as the sacred mountain. The differences of opinion as to location do not affect the historical reality of the mountain nor the certainty that at its base there took place the most important event in the history of the Hebrew people.

The Sinaitic Covenant. At the foot of Sinai and in the midst of grandly impressive manifestations of Jehovah, Israel entered into solemn covenant relations with Him. It was a covenant of blood and was the most sacred and inviolable ceremony known to the ancient peoples. Half of the blood was sprinkled on the alter and half upon the people, thus signifying that all had consented to the terms of the covenant. In this covenant Israel is obligated to loyalty, service and worship, while Jehovah is to continue to protect and deliver them. This covenant is commonly called "The Law of Moses." All the rest of the Old Testament is a development of this fundamental law and shows the application of it in the experience of Israel.

The Purpose of the Mosaic Law. It should be observed that the rewards and punishments of this law were mainly confined to this life. Instead of leading them to believe that outward obedience to it would bring personal salvation and, therefore, instead of superseding the plan of salvation through a redeemer, that had been announced to Adam and Eve, and confirmed in the covenant with Abraham, it pointed to the

Savior. The sacrifices foreshadowed the substitution of the Lamb of God as a means of their deliverance for sin and its punishment.

There are probably two purposes in promulgating this law. (1) To preserve the Israelites as a separate and peculiar people. To the weld the scattered fugitives from Egypt into a nation, distinct from other nations, required laws that would make them different in customs, religion and government. (2) A second purpose was to provide additional spiritual light, that they might know the way of salvation more perfectly.

The Several Parts of the Law. On the whole the law contains three parts. (1) The Law of Duty. This is given in the form of ten commandments (Ex. ch. 20) and relates to individual obligations, (a) The first four define one's obligations to God. (b) The fifth defines our relation to parents, (c) The last five define our relation to the other members of society. These ten words define religion in terms of life and deed as well as worship. They reach the very highest standard and, in the last command, trace crime back to the motive even to the thought in the mind of man. They point out duties arising out of the unchangeable distinctions of right and wrong.

(2) The law of Mercy. This law is found in the instructions concerning the priesthood and the sacrifices. Through these were seen; (a) the need of an atonement for the sinner's guilt; (b) the need of inward cleansing on the part of all; (c) the redemption of the forfeited life of the sinner by another life being substituted in its stead and only by that means; (d) the fact that God would punish wrong-doing and reward righteousness. This is also called "The Law of Holiness" or "The Ceremonial Law" and was intended to show Israel man's sinfulness and how a sinful people could approach a holy God and themselves become holy. It, therefore, deals with such matters as personal chastity, unlawful marriages and general social purity and the religious behavior by which they were to be absolved from all impurity and symbolically to be made pure again.

(3) The Law of Justice. This is composed of miscellaneous civil, criminal, humane and sanitary laws, calculated to insure right treatment of one another and thus promote the highest happiness of all: (a) There was to be kindness and justice to each other including slaves, and also to domestic animals; This is beautifully shown in the provisions for the treatment of the poor, the aged and the afflicted; (b) The rights of property were to be sacredly regarded and all violations of

such rights severely punished as in the case of fraud or theft; (c) Laws of sanitation and health guarded the imprudent against the contraction of disease and protected the wicked or careless against its spread and thereby saved Israel from epidemics of malignant disease. Thus the right of the innocent and helpless were insured; (d) The sanctity of the home and of personal virtue was held inviolable and every transgressor, such as the man who should commit adultery with another man's wife, was put to death; (e) Life was to be sacred. No man being able to give it was to take it from another and so the murderer was to pay the penalty by giving his life.

These laws were so amplified as to meet every demand of the domestic, social, civic and industrial relations of the nation. There could hardly be designed a happier life than the proper observance of all these laws would have brought to Israel. This legislation reached its noblest expression in the law of the neighbor: "Thou shall love thy neighbor as thyself" (Lev. 19:18). It is the final word in all right relation to others.

The Journey to Kadesh-Barnea. After camping before Sinai a little more than a year, during which tune they received the law and were gradually organized into a nation, the cloud by which they were always led from the time of their departure to their entrance to Canaan, arose from the tabernacle and set forward. It led them by a way that we cannot now trace but which Moses says was eleven days' journey from the sacred mountain. (Dt. 1:2).

A few notable events of this journey are recorded. (1) The fire of Jehovah that burned in the camp because of their murmuring. (2) The appointing of seventy elders to share with Moses the burden of the people. (3) The sending of the quails and the destruction of those that lusted. (4) Miriam, the sister of Moses, was smitten with leprosy because with Aaron she rebelled against Moses and spoke disrespectfully of him.

The Twelve Spies. From Kadesh Moses sent out twelve men who should investigate the condition of Canaan. These men agreed that it was an attractive and well favored land. They brought back evidences of its fruitfulness. Only two of them, believed they could conquer it. The People yielded to the opinions of the majority and refused to attempt to enter Canaan and even worse they openly resolved to return to Egypt. For this disbelief and open rebellion they were sentenced to wander forty years in the wilderness and all of them who were above twenty years old except Joshua and Caleb were not only doomed not to be allowed to enter this promised land but were to die in the wilderness.

Lessons of the Period. The more important truths taught by the records of this period may be divided into three groups. (1) Those about man and his nature: (a) He is sinful, his whole nature is out of proper attitude toward God and is a fountain of evil; (b) He is, therefore, in need of redemption and cannot have the benefit of worship to God without it; (c) He owes obedience to God. (2) There are lessons about God: (a) He is shown to be a Holy God. who hates and punishes sin; (b) He is represented as a God of mercy and forgiveness; (c) He is seen as one of power and might, able to carry forward his plans and to change the whole destiny of a people. (3) There is a many sided view of redemption: (a) It is based on blood; The victim must shed its blood before redemption can come; (b) It is by Institution as is attested by all the sacrifices; (c) It is by imputation or the putting of one's sins upon the victim; (d) It is by death and that of an innocent creature. In all of this there is a revelation of Christ who puts away sin and brings the sinner into favor with God.

For Study and Discussion. (1) The awe-inspiring ways by which Jehovah made known his presence on Sinai. (2) The several things Israel covenanted to do. (3) The worship of the golden calf and the breaking of the tables of stone. (4) The three great divisions of the law. (5) The law of mercy or of Holiness, what it teaches, and its purpose. (6) Catalogue the different laws of justice according to the outline suggested above or make a new outline and catalogue them. (7) The present day conditions that could be met and changed for good by an application of these laws. (8) The tabernacle and its material. (9) The different kinds of offering, learn what was offered and how and by whom. (10) The different scared occasions, feasts, holidays, etc. (11) The different occasions of rebellion on the part of the people and what resulted. (12) The spirit of Moses as seen in his talks to the people and in his prayers to God. (13) The rebellion of Miriam and Aaron against Moses. (14) The results of wrong influences or reports as seen in the case of the spies. (15) The rewards of righteousness as seen in the entire period.

Chapter VII

From Kadesh to the Death of Moses.

Num. 14-Dt. 34.

The Pathos of the Forty Years. The stories of this period have running through them an element of pathos arising especially from two sources. (1) Perhaps the experiences of Moses are most sorrowful. That he should now, after faithfully bringing this people to the very border of the land which they sought, be compelled to spend forty monotonous years in this bare and uninteresting desert must have been a disappointment very heavy to bear. During these wanderings he buried Miriam, his sister, and Aaron, his brother and helper. He was often complained of by the people he was trying to help, and because of it was led to sin in such a way as to cause God to refuse him the privilege of entering Canaan. It was necessary for him to appoint his successor and himself be buried in these lands. He was compelled to renumber the people to find that all but two of those who were above twenty when they left Egypt had perished. (2) Surely the experience of the people of Israel during these years is sufficient to arouse a feeling of pity. Forty years of suffering and unhappiness and the loss of all opportunity to enter Canaan by those who fell in the wilderness beclouds the whole story.

The Events of the Forty Years' Wandering. It is now impossible to trace exactly any except the latter portion of their journeyings. It is clear that they went from place to place, not of course marching continuously each day, but changing their location as often at least as the requirements of pasturage demanded. Of the early portion of these years we know but little. They seemed to have remained a long while at Kadesh (Dt. 1:45) and indeed may have made it a sort of headquarters. The story of the rebellion of Konah with the consequent punishment, and the budding of Aarons rod by which the appointment of the family of Aaron to the priesthood was attested are the important incidents of this period.

36

Final Scenes at Kadesh. After about thirty-eight years had elapsed (Dt. 2:14), and the period of wandering was nearly at an end, Israel is again found at Kadesh (Num. 20:11) on the borders of Edom where the spies had been sent out and they made their calamitous blunder. Here at this time happened three important events; (1) Miriam died and was buried, (2) Moses smote the rock and brought forth water, but because he smote it instead of speaking to it Jehovah was angry with him and told him he should not enter the land of promise. (3) Moses asked permission of the King of Edom to pass peaceably through his land and was refused. They were, therefore, compelled to take a long journey around Edom to reach there own land.

From Kadesh to the Jordan. When they were refused passage through the land of the Edomites, their kinsmen, (Num. 20:14-21), the Hebrews made a long journey around. On this journey occurred three important events. (1) The death of Aaron in Mount Hor (Num. 20:22-29). (2) The defeat of the King of South Canaan and the laying waste of his country to Hormah where they had been routed nearly forty years ago. (3) The sending of the fiery serpents and the brazen serpent as a remedy. They also passed the country of Moab and came finally to the river Arnan (Num. 21:13), which is the boundary between Moab and the Amorites. Here they came into conflict with Sihon the King of the Amorites, whom they defeated, and possessed his land. (Num. 21:23-24). The overcoming of this strong and ancient people brought Israel into contact with Og, king of Bashan, who was himself a giant and whose country was far more formidable than that of the Amorites. By defeating him and possessing his cities Israel was enabled to pass on and come to the plains of Moab beyond Jordan at Jericho. In Psalms 135 and 136, written hundreds of years later, the victory over Sihon and Og and the overthrow of Pharaoh are dwelt on together in such a way as to show that their conquest was regarded as an achievement worthy to rank along side of that of their deliverance from the power of Egypt.

The Prophecies of Balaam. (Num. Chaps. 22-24). The Moabites were greatly distressed about the settlement of the victorious Hebrews in the region just north of them and feared lest they should suffer the same fate as Shihon and Og. Balak, the King of Moab, had beard of Balaam, a famous soothsayer or wise prophet of Chaldea, whose curses and blessings were reported to carry with them extraordinary effects. He sought at any cost to have him cripple Israel by placing a curse upon them. But instead of cursing Israel and blessing the Moabites, he revealed how wonderfully Israel was blessed Of God and how a scepter would rise out of Israel and smite and destroy Moab.

This strange man Balaam seems to have had the gift of prophecy without its grace. He had the knowledge of future events but sought to use it for his own advantage instead of for the glory of God. He was a covetous, money-loving prophet and sought the rewards offered by Balak. He tried repeatedly to find some way by which he could speak good for Moab and thereby earn the much desired fee. On the other hand he was afraid to speak against Israel lest the curse should recoil on him. No other word seems to describe his course except to say that he was compelled by Jehovah to speak to Israel's advantage and to predict her future greatness. His language fittingly describes the material splendor and the splendid victories and reign of David. The spirit of Israel described is that of the united kingdom standing at the zenith of its power. In a beautiful way also he pointed to the Messiah who should put all enemies under his feet.

He may have secured his reward, however, in another way. He seems to have led Balak to entice Israel, through pretensions of friendship, to partake in the idolatrous and impure festivals of the Moabites (Num. 25:1-5; 31:15-16; Rev. 2:14). These and other acts of their own brought down upon Israel the curse of heaven and made them the subject of such calamites as Balaam could not himself pronounce against them. By suggesting this course to Balak, he may have obtained the coveted pay without directly disobeying God. This whole story would seem to imply that the Hebrew historians did not believe that divine relations were limited to seers and prophets of their own race.

The Last Acts of Moses. Events are now transpiring in rapid succession and the story hastens to the close of the career of Moses, the great leader prophet, priest and judge of Israel. Several matters are worthy of study: (1) The sending of an expedition to destroy the Midianites. (2) The final numbering of the people preparatory to their entrance into Canaan. (3) The appointing of Joshua as his successor. (4) The settlement of the two and a half tribes on the east side of Jordan. (5) The appointment of the cities of refuge. (8) The delivery of a farewell address, or of farewell addresses.

The Last Scene on Moab. There were far too many of the Israelites to hear his voice and he probably gathered together the princes and elders who listened to him from day to day, each of whom went home and repeated to his own people what he had heard from their inspired leader. In these addresses Moses recounted their wanderings and Jehovah's goodness to them. He reminded them of all that God had commanded them in his law and gave such new instructions and interpretations as would be needed in the new conditions that they would meet on coming into the Promised Land. He painted in frightful colors the fearful doom that would befall the disobedient and eloquently described the blessing of loyalty to God. After being called of God to depart into the mountains and die, he pronounced in one of the most beautiful passages in all the scripture, his farewell blessing upon each of the tribes.

And how solemn must have been the occasion. They are listening for the last time to his voice. With what veneration they must have gazed on him. He it was that Jochebed with loving hands had laid in the bulrushes when 120 years ago Pharaoh had persecuted them. He was the man that had so nobly chosen to suffer affliction with the people of God instead of the attractions of Egypt. His eyes under the shadow of Horeb had looked on the burning bush. His hand had stretched out over Egypt and overwhelmed it with the plagues. His was the face that had reflected the divine glory of the mount after forty days of fellowship with Jehovah, during which he received the substance of the law. That was the faithful and tried man that had often been wrongly accused, that had meekly borne so many trials, that had guided the people so faithfully, and advised them so wisely, and had refused honors himself because he loved them so well. How they must have hung on those last words! And the echo of his last words had hardly died away until his spirit had been called away and unseen hands had laid his dust in an unknown tomb.

The Significance of the Work of Moses. Humanly speaking, he explains the great difference between the Hebrews and the people kindred to them. He accounts for their development from a company of disheartened slaves, and from the careless habits of wandering tribes into a conquering nation, made irresistible by its belief in the guidance of Jehovah. Humanly speaking, he was the creator of Israel. (1) He was a leader and as such heartened and disciplined them. (2) He was a prophet and as such taught them ideals of social justice, purity and honor. (3) He was a lawgiver and as such furnished them with civil, sanitary, social and religious laws that channeled them into a sober, healthy, moral, and right-minded people. (4) He was the founder of a religion and as such led them into a real loyalty to Jehovah as their God and gave them such a conception of the divine character and requirements as to stimulate in them a growth in goodness.

Lessons of the Period. The student will readily collect for himself lessons that have been brought to his attention. The following, however, should not fail of consideration: (1) God's law is inflexible. It is of universal operation and can not be evaded or revoked. Even the best men must suffer if they violate it as was the case of Moses. (2) To rebel against God's appointed leaders and to speak disrespectfully of them will subject one to the outpouring of divine wrath. (3) God never forgets his covenants as seen In the case of his refusal to give to Israel the land of Edom and of Ammon. (4) That God decides the fate of armies in battle and is therefore the God of nations as well as individuals. (5) Early hardships often fit us for a more glorious destiny later.

For Study and Discussion. (1) The rebellion of Korah. (2) The story of Balak and Balaam and the present day truth which it suggests or the problems of today to which it is applicable. (3) The story of the budding of Aaron's rod. (4) The sin of Moses because of which he was not allowed to enter Canaan. Find every reference to it. (5) The different victories of Israel recorded in the period. (6) The fiery serpents and serpent of brass. (7) The cities of refuge, their names, location, purpose and the lessons for today to be drawn from their use. (8) The principal events of Israel's past history mentioned in Dt. chs. 1-4, and find where in previous books each is recorded. (9) From Dt. chs. 27-28 list the curses and blessings, showing the sin and its penalty and the blessing and that for which it is promised. (10) The farewell blessing of Moses on the tribes (Dt. ch. 33). List the promises to each. (11) The death of Moses (Dt. chs. 32 and 34). (12) The incidents of the period that have in them a miraculous element. (13) Other prominent leaders besides Moses, Aaron and Joshua. (14) The nations mentioned with whom the Hebrews had contact. (15) The geography of the places and nations noticed in this period.

Chapter VIII

Joshua's Conquest.

Joshua.

The Facts of History Recorded. The history recorded in this period follows closely upon and completes the story of the deliverance begun in the Exodus. But for the sin of Israel in believing the evil spies and turning back into the wilderness, none of the events of the last twenty-one chapters of Numbers and none of those found in Deuteronomy would have occurred and Joshua would have followed Exodus and have completed the story of Israel's deliverance out of Egypt into Canaan. As it is, this history follows close upon that of Deuteronomy. Joshua, who had been duly chosen and set apart for the work, took command of the hosts as soon as Moses died. He was trained in the school of Moses and exhibited the same devotion to Jehovah and the same dependence upon His guidance.

The Story Naturally Falls Into Three Parts. (1) The conquest of Canaan, (Chs. 1-12). In this section we have the story of the crossing of the Jordan, fall of Jericho and the conquest of the land both south and north. (2) The division of the territory of Canaan (Chs. 13-22). In this section we have the assignment of the territory of Canaan, the cities of Refuge, the cities of Levites and the return of the two and half tribes to the east of the Jordan. (3) Joshua's last counsel and death (Chs. 23-24), in which we have his exhortations to fidelity and farewell address and death.

While the war itself probably did not continue but seven years, the entire period was not less than twenty-five and may have been as much as fifty-one years. The period marks a new era in Biblical history. Instead of the experiences of Nomadic or semi-Nomadic tribes, a people with a fixed abode and with a growing body of customs and institutions is described.

The Land of Canaan. It is well to consider at least three things concerning this little, yet wonderful country. (1) Its geography. It is

41

about four hundred miles long and from seventy-five to one hundred miles wide and is made up of plains, valleys, plateaus, gorges and mountains fashioned together in wonderful variety. There are many small bodies of land capable of supporting a group of people and yet so secluded as to allow them to develop their own individuality and become independent. Every traveler between Egypt and Babylonia must pass through Palestine which thereby became the bridge for the civilization and commerce of tie world. Here the Hebrew could easily keep in touch with the world events of his day. Later it became the gateway of travel from east to west. The territory naturally falls into three divisions: (a) Judah or Judea which is in the southern portion and about seventy-five miles long, (b) Ephraim or Samaria occupying the center of the country, (c) Galilee occupying the northern portion. Along the entire coast line there is a continuous coast plain. There are many mountains, the most important being Hermon, Carmel and Gerizim.

(2) Its inhabitants and the nations surrounding it. That the population was very dense is indicated by the mention of about three hundred cities and towns a large number of which have been identified. While there were many war-like people crowded into Palestine, seven, the Hittites, the Girgashites, the Perizzites, the Hivites, the Jebusites, the Amorites and the Canaanites, were the most important. The Canaanites, who had been there about six centuries, and the Amorites, who had lived there about ten centuries, were the two peoples that furnished greatest resistance to Israel's occupancy of the country. They were virtually one people.

Around Palestine were many kingdoms, some large and strong, some small and weak. Among the more important were the Philistines, west of Judah, the Phoenician kingdoms on the north, Arameans or Syrians on the northeast, and on the east and southeast, the Ammonites, Moabites and Edomites, the last three being kinsmen of the Hebrews.

(3) Conditions favorable to its conquest. Several circumstances conspired to make it a suitable time for the Hebrews to enter Canaan: (a) Egypt had crushed the Hittites and devastated their land; (b) Northern hordes from and through Syria had broken the power of Egypt and the Hittites and had also crushed the Canaanites; (c) Assyria had increased her borders to the coasts of Phoenicia and was feared by

42

all other peoples; (d) Babylonia was not strong enough to displace Assyria as an Asiatic power but strong enough to dispute her supremacy; (e) For two hundred years, therefore, their weakness together with that of Egypt and the Hittites gave the Hebrews ample time to develop and grow strong.

The Crossing of the Jordan and the Fall of Jericho. To the Hebrews these two incidents have always been of first importance. As the two great events through which they gained entrance to their permanent home, they have been given a place in Hebrew literature almost equal to that of their deliverance from Egyptian bondage. The divine share in these great accomplishments was fully recognized. He it was who caused the waters of Jordan to separate and He it was who threw down the walls of Jericho. Not only did Jericho occupy a strategic position, being somewhat apart from other Canaanite cities, but the marvelous manner of its fall both encouraged the Hebrews to expect complete victory and also caused the Canaanites to fear them and expect defeat.

The Complete Conquest of Canaan. The conquest was a sort of whirlwind campaign that crushed the active and dangerous opposition of the Canaanites, the complete occupancy being accomplished by a piecemeal process of subduing one after another of the little cities and independent tribes. The campaign was well planned. The Jordan was crossed, Jericho was taken and then by pushing forward for the heart of the land, Ai was overcome and in a short time Joshua was in the center of the land, ready to strike either way. With his central camp established at Gilgal (5:10; 9:6) and the forces of Canaan divided, Joshua could advance by two lines of invasion. Whether he made simultaneous campaigns in different directions is not certain, but he seems first to have turned his attention to the southern territory and then to have completed his conquest by an invasion of the northern districts. After bending before this storm the Canaanites still held possession of the land and the piecemeal process of subjugation began. It was not all accomplished by the sword but aided by the peaceful measures of inter-marriage and treaties with friendly neighbors. Israel contended against a far superior civilization but finally won because the religious as well as the civil and social life was involved.

The Cruelty to the Canannites. Stress has commonly been laid on the cruelty to the Canaanites and upon their being driven out of their

43

land when it should have been put upon their character where the Scripture puts it. This is a waste of false sympathy. The Scripture always speaks of the driving out of the Canaanites as a punishment for their sins (Dt, 9:4-5; Lev. 18:24-25). Some of the abominations which they practiced are described in Lev. 18:21-30 and Dt. 12:30-32. These abominations were practiced in the name of religion and were so shocking that one shudders to read the description.

Everything evil was worshiped. The chief god was Baal, the sun, who was worshiped at different places under different names, but everywhere his worship was fierce and cruel. His consort Ashtaroth, the Babylonian goddess Istar, the goddess of love, worshiped as the morning star, Venus, fostered in her worship abominations that are almost inconceivable in our times. It was a worship of impurity and could not be cured by ordinary means. God had borne with it for hundreds of years. Their destruction was therefore justifiable just as was that of the old world and the Jews were simply God's instruments just as were the waters of the flood or the fire and brimstone in the case of Sodom and Gomorrah.

God was planning to begin, a new nation, to start a new civilization and by using this method of punishment for the Canaanites he impressed the Hebrews in a most striking way with the consequences of forsaking worship of the true God. It was a new thing in the world to have all idolatrous symbols destroyed and to worship an unseen God and yet Joshua constantly represented to them that all the evils they had inflicted upon the Canaanites, and greater evils, would be sent upon them if they should become idolaters. Little, therefore, need be said of the cruelty of the Hebrews nor of the suffering of the Canaanites. The Hebrews were the instrument of God and the Canaanites were reaping what they had sown.

The Significance of the War Against the Canannites. Of all the wars recorded in human history this was one of the greatest, if not the greatest of all. None was ever fought for a more noble purpose and none has accomplished greater ends. The fate of the world was in the balance. Old civilizations on account of their wickedness, were to soon fall and this series of conflicts was to decide whether a new civilization with a pure and holy purpose to serve God could arise in their midst. It was, therefore, a war (1) For purification. The individual, the temple and the home must all be pure. (2) For civil liberty. Israel was now, under God, to govern herself and thereby to give the world a pattern of government as God's free nation. (3) For religious liberty. Idolatry, vice and superstition were everywhere and the people must be free to worship the one true God and Creator of all. (4) For the whole world. Israel was to be a blessing to all nations. Out of her and out of this land was to come Christ, her son, who should save the nations. The war was, therefore, for us as well as for them.

The Character and Work of Joshua. The name Joshua in the Old Testament is equivalent to Jesus in the New (Heb. 4:8). His character and work were well adapted to his age and he therefore made a deep impression upon this formative period of Israel's history. He was fully prepared for the work of the conquest by his association with Moses and by such events as the defeat of Amalek which he accomplished by divine help (Ex. 17:10-16). With all he had been called of God and set apart for the work of subjugating the Canaanites. As a soldier and commander, he ranks among the first of the world. He is resourceful, brave, straightforward, fertile in strategy, and quick to strike (1:10-11; 2:1 etc.). In the councils of peace he was wise and generous. He displayed statesmanship of the highest order in mapping out the boundaries of the tribes and thus preparing the land for a permanent occupancy of the Hebrews. In the matter of religion he was actuated by a spirit of implicit obedience to God's authority. He combined in his nature both courage and gentleness and exhibited in his dealings the disposition of both the lion and the lamb. His dying charge is full of earnestness and devotion. As a type of Christ he led the people to the "rest" of Canaan, though not to the rest of the gospel which "remaineth to the people of God." A void still remained and they still had to look forward. He led them to victory over their enemies and became their advocate when they sinned and met defeat.

Lessons of the Period. Among many lessons suggested by this book the following should be considered and the student asked to suggest others. (1) God is at war with sin: (a) He thrusts out the Canaanites because of their sins; (b) He allows the defeat of Israel at Ai because sin was among them; (c) He allows Achan put to death because of it. He is, therefore, against all sin, personal, social and civic or national. (2) Religious victory and entrance upon spiritual rest is accomplished

45

through a leader or commander and through a divine power, not through a law giver and by the works of the law. It was not Moses, the lawgiver, through whom they entered and not by their own strength. (3) God keeps his covenants in spite of all the weakness of man. (4) God decides the issues of battles and of wars with a view to the final on-going of his kingdom. Only God and not the relative strength or preparedness of the contending armies can forecast the final issues of war. (5) The fact that God is for one does not preclude the use of strategy and discretionary methods. (6) The failure or sin of one man may defeat a whole cause and that in spite of the faithful efforts of many others. (7) What is a just severity to some is often a great mercy to others. The destruction of the Canaanites was a severe penalty for their sins, but it was an unspeakable blessing to all the future ages because by it a true faith and a pure worship was preserved.

For Study and Discussion. (1) Each of the lessons suggested above. Find a basis either in incident or teaching for each. (2) The geography of the country with the principal cities mentioned. (3) The several tribes of people mentioned in the narrative. (4) The providential conditions favorable to the conquest just at that time. (5) The cruelties of the Israelites to their enemies. Select examples and discuss each. (6) The significance of the war. (7) The character and work of Joshua. Point out incidents or acts that show elements of greatness and weakness in his character; also estimate the value of his work. (8) The cooperation of the two and a half tribes in these wars. (9) The several battles described. List them and decide what contributed to the success or failure of Israel in each case. (10) The story of the fall of Jericho. (11) The sin of Achan, its results, its discovery and punishment. (12) The story of the Gibeonites, their stratagem, its embarrassment to Joshua and consequent slavery to them. (13) The portion of land allotted to each tribe and how it was secured. (14) The miraculous element running through the narrative. List and discuss each incident that tends to show or makes claim of such miraculous element. (15) The place of prayer and worship in the hook. Give incidents. (16) The element that is figurative or illustrative of truth revealed in New Testament times.

Chapter IX

The Judges.

Judges 1; 1 Sam. 7.

The Characteristics of the Times. This is a period of transition for Israel Nothing was quite certain, and "every man did that which was right in his own eyes" (17:6). In consequence of this there was lack of organization, cooperation or leadership. While we do not have all the history covered by the period and while we do not easily understand or explain its events, it is clear that things did not run smoothly. In Judges 2:16-19 the author gives a vivid picture of the conditions and characteristics of the time. The problems of the times may be outlined as follows: (1) Political problems. These arose, (a) because of the isolated conditions of the tribes, (b) because of their tribal government which lacked the bond of unity of former times, (c) because of the strength and opposition of the Canaanites. (2) Social problems. These grew out of: (a) the adoption of Canaanite customs and manner of life, (b) the intermarriage of the Jews with the new people. (3) Religious Problems. The source of these problems arose from two directions, (a) Baal worship ministered to their lusts and was therefore a snare to them, (b) the religion of Israel required purity and was, therefore, counted a burden. The problems of the times of peace were greater than those in the times of war.

The Judges. Now that there was no central stable government and no hereditary rulers the people accepted from time to time as their rulers certain military leaders whom God raised up and who, by their prowess, delivered them from the yoke of foreign oppression. It was, therefore, a period of personal efforts some of which are preserved for us in this portion of scripture. Fifteen Judges are named counting Eli and Samuel, who are by some not so named, but we know very little of any except six of the military judges and Eli and Samuel. These six are brought into prominence because of as many invasions by other nations as follows. (1) The Mesopotamians came down from the northeast and oppressed Israel until Othniel, Caleb's nephew, was raised up to deliver them. (2) The invasion of the Moabites and the deliverance through Ehud. (3) The oppression of the Canaanites, who came down from the north, was thrown off through the leadership of Deborah assisted by Barak. (4) The Midianites came in from the east and greatly oppressed Israel until Gideon defeated and destroyed these bold oppressors. (5) The invasion of the Ammonites and Israel's deliverance through Jephthah. (6) The Philistines were the next successful enemies of Israel and were enabled to do great harm to Israel until Samson arose and overthrew their power.

Eli and Samuel differed widely from the other judges and on that account are sometimes not counted among them. Eli was a good but weak man. His weakness in the control of his children ruined them and brought him to sorrow and also caused a severe defeat for Israel.

Samuel was the last of the judges and was also a priest and prophet. He is one of the outstanding Old Testament characters. Abraham founded the Hebrew race; Joseph saved them from famine; Moses gave them a home and Samuel organized them into a great kingdom which led to their glory. His birth was in answer to prayer and as judge or deliverer he won his most signal victory, that against the Philistines, by means of prayer. He founded schools for the instruction of young prophets at Gilgal. Bethel, Mizpeh and Ramah. In this he perhaps rendered his most valuable and most lasting service. These schools gave a great impetus to prophecy. After this time prophecy and prophets had a vital and permanent place in the life of the nation. Even kings had to consult them for instructions from God.

Ruth the Moabite. In contrast with the many stories of idolatry and sin of the times and especially in contrast with the story of the idolatry of Micah and the crime of Gibeah found in the last chapters of Judges, we have the beautiful little story of Ruth, the Moabite. Others had turned away from Jehovah the true God to false gods, but she turned from the false gods and received the true God.

Other Nations. Of the condition of the other nations of this period we are left largely to the monuments, but much has been discovered that throws light on the general world conditions. The following might be noted here. (1) Egypt. After the Exodus of Israel Egypt seems to have enjoyed several centuries of great prosperity during which the country

48

was adorned with wonderful buildings, her religion prospered, her people were famous for their learning and, through colonization projects, she carried her civilization to many other climes. (2) Assyria was now a growing empire and destined to become, ere long, one of the most powerful of all. (3) Babylonia was now weak and generally at a disadvantage in contests with other nations. (4) The Elamites also became a people of considerable influence and at least on different occasions invaded Babylonia. (5) Mesopotamia, before being absorbed by Assyria was a powerful nation and ravaged Syria and Palestine. (6) Phoenicia was a country of great commercial progress with Tyre and Sidon as centers of great influence. (7) Greece. The most interesting of all the countries that began to show their strength during that period is Greece. The inhabitants were wonderful in physical energy, in war and conquest, in discovery and in capacity for education. They were fond of pleasure and had great capacity for the tasks of society, government, and religion. They contrived a religious system that was conspicuous for the absence of the great priestly class of the eastern systems of religion. However, it left the morally corrupt nature of man untouched and, therefore, did not contribute anything to the cause of pure religion.

Outline of The Narrative. The Scripture narrative falls into the following well-defined divisions: (1) An introduction or the condition in Palestine at the beginning of the period, Jud. 1:1-3:6. (2) The Judges and their work, Jud. 3:1:1-3:6. (2) The Judges and their work, (Jud. 3:7-16 end). (3) Micah's idolatry, Jud. Chs. 17-18. (4) The crime of Gibeah, Jud. Chs. 19-21. (5) The story of Ruth, Ruth. (6) The career of Samuel including the judgeship of Eli, 1 Sam. Chs. 1-7.

Ethical and Religious Standards. Since this is a transitional period we may expect great difference of moral and religions standards. Some things are stressed far beyond their importance while other matters of more consequence are overlooked. The following examples will indicate to what extremes they went in some matters. (1) Some things bad: (a) Murdering a heathen enemy was counted a virtue; (b) It was not a crime to steal from a member of another Hebrew tribe; (c) Might was right; (d) They would keep any foolish vow to God even though it cost the life of one's child as in the case of Jephthah. (2) Some things good: (a) The marriage relation was held sacred; (b) A covenant was held binding and sacred as in the case of the Gibeonites; (c) They

49

.

counted inhospitality a crime. (3) Some strange inconsistencies: (a) Micah would steal his mother's silver, then rear a family altar to Jehovah; (b) Samson would keep his Nazarite vow, preserve his hair intact and abstain from wine and unclean food but give himself over to lying and to his passions, and selfish inclinations and fail to observe the simple laws of justice, mercy and service.

Lessons of the Period. (1) As to national decay: (a) It is caused by religious apostasy; (b) It evidences itself in religious blindness, political folly and social immorality; (c) Its curse results in political and social disorder, chaos and ultimate ruin. (2) As to punishment for sin: (a) He surely sends punishment on the offender whether an individual or a nation; (b) His punishment is a matter of mercy and is intended to prepare the way for deliverance. (3) As to deliverance: (a) It never comes until repentance is manifested; (b) It is always through a deliverer whom we can not find but whom God must raise up for us. (4) From the book of Ruth it is shown that circumstances neither make nor mar believers.

For Study and Discussion. (1) The names of the Judges in order with the length of time each served or the period of rest after the work of each. (2) The enemy each judge had to combat. (3) What each judge accomplished against the enemy and what weapon he used-an oxgoad or what? (4) The elements of strength and weakness in the character of the principal men of the period. (5) The New Testament truths illustrated in the life and work of Gideon and Samson. (6) The lessons of practical life illustrated by the stories of Jephthah and Deborah. (7) The facts of the story of Micah and Gibeah. (8) The career of Samuel as found so far. (9) The value of a trusting soul as seen in Ruth. (10) The main element in their religion. (11) The condition of Israel at the beginning and at the end of this period. (12) The subject of good and successful parents with bad and unsuccessful children. The importance they attached to the Ark of the Covenant.

Chapter X

The Reign of Saul.

I Sam. 8-31; I Chron. 10

The Demand for a King. The last period saw one tribe after another come to the front and assert itself through some leading man as an emergency arose, but now the tribes are to be united into a monarchy and this, too, at their own request made in the form of a desire for a king. Several things no doubt influenced them to make this request. (1) From the days of Joshua there had been no strong national bond. They were only held together by the law of Moses and the annual assemblages at Shiloh. But the wise reign of Samuel had given an enlarged national consciousness and led to a desire for a stable government with the largest possible national unity. (2) The failure of the sons of Samuel, who had been entrusted with some power and who would naturally succeed him, led them to feel that provision for the welfare of the nation must be made before the death of Samuel or ruin would come. (3) The attitude of the nations around Israel suggested the need of a strong government headed by a leader of authority. The Philistines and Ammonites had already made incursions into their land and threatened at any time to further oppress them. The new organization, therefore, seemed necessary as a national protection. (4) The faith of Jehovah was threatened. The victories of the Philistines would be interpreted to mean that Jehovah was powerless or else did not care for his people. This would lead them to turn to other gods. Then too they were greatly tempted by the religion of the Canaanite to turn from Jehovah. It was, therefore, a religious crisis that made it essential that the Hebrews unite and in the name of Jehovah over throw the Philistines and establish a nation that would rightly represent to all nations Jehovah as the God of their race. (5) The nations around them such as Egypt and Assyria with their seats of royalty had excited their pride and they were moved with a desire to be like their heathen neighbors-a desire which involved disrespect for their divine king and want of faith in him.

The Principle of the Kingdom. The folly of the people did not lie in their asking for a king to rule over them, but in the spirit of forgetfulness of God with which they made the request. Indeed Moses had provided for a kingdom and given the law upon which the king was to rule (Dt 17:14-20). He was to be unlike other kings. He was not to rule according to his own will or that of the people but according to the will of Jehovah. He was to be subject to God as was the humblest Israelite, and, under his immediate direction, was to rule for the good of the people. This was a new principle that showed it self in all the future history of Israel. Saul attempted to be like others-to assert his own will-and disobeyed God and was deposed while David identified himself with God and his purposes and was successful. One represent the ideal of the people, the other that of the Scripture.

Saul the First King. He began his career under the most auspicious circumstances. His tribe and its location as well as his fine physical appearance gave him great advantage. He was enthusiastic and brave, and yet in the early days he charms us with his modesty. After he was anointed by Samuel and had been made to see the great career opening to him he returned to his regular toil until the people were called together at Mizpah and proclaimed him king. Samuel supported him with his influence and the people gave him allegiance. He was for a while subservient to the will of God and greatly prospered. But later he became self-willed and failed to see that the nation was God's and not his. He developed a spirit of disobedience, perverseness and evil conduct that mark him as insane.

Saul's Great Achievements. The oppression of Israel's enemies which in part at least made necessary their king had to be dealt with at once. In his contest with them Saul had a very successful military career. He was successful in the following campaigns: (I) Against the Ammonites (I Sam. 11) in which he delivered from ruin the inhabitants of Jabesh-Gilead on the east Of Jordan and won the love of all the Hebrew people. (2) Against the Philistines (I Sam. 13-14) in which Jonathan was the hero. Before the battle he disobeyed the will of God by performing the duties of a priest and was told he should lose his kingdom on account of it. At the close of the campaign he lost his temper and proposed to kill Jonathan, his son, the hero of the day because he had unwittingly disobeyed a foolish command. (3) Against Moab, Ammon, Edom and Zobah (I Sam. 14:47) of which there are no particulars given. (4) Against the Amalekites (I Sam. 15) in which, though he defeated Amalek, he disobeyed God in not wholly destroying all Amalek and his possessions and thereby lost for the time being Samuel's help and finally his kingdom. It was after this battle that David was anointed to become king in Saul's stead.

Saul's Decline. From Chapter 16 on the story tells of the rapid decline of Saul and of the rise of David to the kingdom. (1) There is given the story of the madness of Saul and the introduction of David to the court as the king's musician. (2) The campaign against the Philistines in which David kills Goliath, the giant that was defying Israel, and won great honor from the king. (3) His effort to destroy David. During many years he, with bitter jealousy and an insane hatred, tried to destroy David who was as constantly delivered by a divine providence. Whether on account of sickness or other reason, he seems to have had fits of insanity during this period. (4) His last battle and death. The Philistines arrayed themselves against Saul. With a sense of defeat he tried to get in touch with Samuel, but finally met a death in harmony with his life and thus ended one of the most melancholy careers of all history. All because of his disobedience to God (I Chron. 10:1.1-14).

Lessons of the Period. (1) God adapts his methods to the needs and conditions of the people from tribal government to kingdom. (2) A man out of harmony with God will certainly fail-Saul. (3) A man in harmony with God's plan will succeed no matter how much opposed by others-David. (4) God never forgets to punish those who oppress his people-Amalekites. (5) The success of God's work does not depend upon our attitude toward his will, but our condition when it has succeeded does. (6) A righteous man can succeed without doing wrong to do it. (7) God's anointed will suffer if they sin. (8) Kindness to enemies-David to Saul. (9) The strength of true friendship-Jonathan and David.

For Study and Discussion. (1) The condition that led to the establishment of the kingdom. (3) Four statements Samuel made to Saul and four ways by which he tried to impress him with the responsibility to which he was called I Sam. 9:19-10-8. (3) The prophet bands or school of prophets. (4) The story of Jonathan's exploits against Michmash by Saul and his escape, I Sam. 14. (5) The story of David's choice and anointing, I Sam. 16:1-13. (6) The killing of Goliath and defeat of the Philistines. I Sam. Ch. 17. (7) Story of Jonathan and David, I Sam. 18:1-4; 19:1-7; 20:1-4, 12-17, 41-42; 23:16-18. (8) David's wanderings, 21:10-22-5. (9) Compare Saul and David at the time of the anointing of each as to their chances of success. (10) David's sojourn in Philistia with the experience of embarrassment and advantage, I Sam. Chs. 27-28. (11) Saul's last battle and death, (a) the appeal to Samuel through the witch, I Sam. Ch. 28, (b) the battle, his and his son's death, I Sam. Ch.31.

Chapter XI

The Reign of David.

2 Sam.; 1 Chron. Chs. 11-29; 1 K 1:1-2:11.

His Reign over Judah. The reign of David is divided into two parts. The first part was over Judah, with the capitol at Hebron, and lasted seven and one-half years. During this period Ishbosheth, son of Saul, reigned over Israel in the North. It is probable that both of these kings were regarded as vassals of the Philistines and paid tribute. On account of rival leaders, there was constant warfare between these two rival kings. The kingdom of Judah, however, gradually gained the ascendancy. This is beautifully described in the Scripture "David waxed stronger and stronger, but the house of Saul waxed weaker and weaker" (2 Sam. 3:1). Seeing this, Abner undertook negotiations looking to the onion of the two kingdoms, but was treacherously killed by Joab. The act of Abner in coming to David was in reality one of secession. It was soon followed by the murder of Ishbosheth and the utter failure of Saul's kingdom.

His Reign Over All Israel. Saul's kingdom having fallen, Israel assembled in great numbers at Hebron and asked David to become king over all the nation. Upon his ascendancy to the throne of the united nations the Philistines sent an army into the Hebrew country. The brief record of these wars shows that they were very bitter and that at one time David was forced to take refuge in the Cave of Adullam and carry on a sort of guerrilla warfare. But finally in the valley of Rephaim he was enabled to strike such a crushing blow to the Philistines as to compel a lasting peace and leave him free to develop his kingdom. This reign of David, lasting thirty-three years after he became king of all, was the ideal reign of all the history of the Hebrews.

The element of success and chief acts of his reign may be summed up somewhat as follows: (1) His capture of Jerusalem (formerly called Jesub,) a Canaanitish stronghold that had resisted all attacks from the days of Joshua, and making it his capitol. This choice showed great wisdom. (2) His foreign relations. David's foreign policy was one of conquest. He not only defended Israel but subdued other nations. Besides the subduing of the Philistines and capture of Jebus, already mentioned, he conquered the Moabites. the Syrians, the Edomites and the Ammonites. He also made an alliance with Hiram, the king of the Phoenicians, who became his lifelong friend. (3) His home relations and policies. His policy at home may be said to be one of centralization. One of his first acts was to bring up the ark and place it on Mount Zion and to center all worship there. This would tend to unite the people and to make more powerful his authority over all the people. In line with this plan he conceived the idea of building the temple and during the years he gathered materials and stored riches with which to build it. He acted with a wise consideration for the rights of his subjects and in every way sought to promote their happiness. As a ruler, he differed very widely from the kings of other countries. He possessed none of their selfish aims. He did not oppress his subjects with heavy taxes, nor spoil them of their possessions, nor seize them for soldiers against their will. He recognized that the king was for the people and not the people for the king.

His Great Sin and Its Bitter Consequences. David's high ideals and noble chivalry could not withstand the enervating influence of his growing harem. The degrading influence of polygamy with its luxury, pleasure seeking and jealousies was soon to undermine his character. His sins and weak indulgencies were destined to work family and national disaster. These sins reached a climax in his trespass with Bathsheba, the wife of Uriah. In this crime he fell from his exalted position to the level of an unprincipled eastern monarch. It stands out as one of the darkest crimes of all history and "shows what terrible remnants of sin there are in the hearts even of converted men". Primitive society followed the course of nature in condemning adultery as worthy of more severe punishment than murder itself. And "no crime today involves more sudden and terrible consequences in the individual; no crime is capable of exerting as malign an influence upon the innocent family and later descendants of the culprit; no crime leaves in its wake as many physical and moral ills."

The Bitter consequences of this sin soon became apparent. Nathan brought to him a worthy rebuke and he showed himself different from other kings of his time by the bitter repentance with which he bewails his iniquity in the fifty-first Psalm. God forgave his sin but its evil consequences in his family and nation could not be removed. The nature of his chastisement is suggested in the following incidents: (1) The death of his child born to Bath-sheba. (2) Ammon, his oldest son, one of the pitiable products of his oriental harem, shamefully treated his sister, Tamar, in the gratification of his brutal lusts. (3) Absalom treacherously murdered Ammon as a matter of revenge for the outrage upon his sister, Tamar. (4) The rebellion of Absalom, his son, which almost cost David the throne and led to the destruction of Absalom. (5) The rebellion of Shebna and following events, which almost destroyed the empire. (6) Many incidents in the family and kingdom of Solomon, his son.

While David must always be judged by the social standards of his age it must be remembered that his own generation did not hesitate to condemn his act and we must not excuse in the least this awful sin. The message it has for us is supremely applicable to our present age in which social evil threatens to undermine our boasted Christian civilization.

The Inspiring Career of David. The life of David is so varied and beautiful that one finds difficulty in outlining any study of him in the space allowed here. There are several ways of studying his career. Sometimes it may be profitable to consider him from two viewpoints, (1) His character, (2) His life after he became king. For our purpose, however, it would be better to look at him somewhat as follows: (1) As a shepherd lad, where he laid the foundations of his great career. (2) As a servant at the court of Saul, where he became the object of a bitter jealousy and suffered great indignities. (3) As a refugee from Saul, during which time he exhibited his unwillingness to do wrong even against one who was doing him great injustice. (4) As a friend, especially shown in his relation to Jonathan. By it he was influenced throughout his whole career and was caused after becoming king to extend kindness to the house of Saul, his enemy. 2 Sam. ch. 9. (5) As a musician. His accomplishments in this field are witnessed both by his ability in the use of the harp and in the great body of psalms which he left us. (6) As a loyal subject. In no other place, perhaps, did he show more fine qualities than in this. To him Saul was God's anointed, and, though wronged by Saul and though himself already anointed to be king in Saul's stead, he remained perfectly loyal to Saul as king. (7) As a ruler. He knew how to govern both his own people and those whom he had subdued. He also succeeded in forming friendly alliances with other kings and changed the enfeebled and divided tribes into a mighty empire. (8) As a military leader. Through his skill he organized a most successful army (1 Chron. 27:1-5; 2 Sam. 23:8-9), and defeated at least five surrounding nations and so impressed the great world powers beyond that they did not oppose the growth of his kingdom. (9) As a servant of God. Though making his mistakes, he was a "man after God's own heart." He made Jerusalem the great center of religion and organized the priests and Levites so that their work could be done effectively and with order. The key-note of his life seems to have been expressed to Goliath (I Sam. 17:45). (10) As a type of Christ. Of all the human types of Jesus in the Old Testament David is probably the most eminent. This fact makes the study of his life and experiences of great interest and profit to the Christian.

His Last Days. The last days of David are made sad because of his own weakness. The memory of his guilt and disgrace had led him to withdraw more and more from the public life and, therefore, to neglect the duties of judge and ruler. His court became the scene of plotting concerning his successor, whose name he had apparently not announced. It was only by the valuable help of Nathan that he succeeded in having his wish in the matter.

The dying words of David have in them much that is prophetic of the Messiah and points out to Solomon, his beloved son, who was to reign in his stead, the way of all success and blessing. It, however, contains what has been designated as "the greatest blot on David's character"-His charge to Solomon to put to death Shimei and Joab. Such vindictiveness does not seem to comport with his spirit manifested in the sparing of Saul in the days of his jealous hatred and in his kindness to the house of Saul (2 Sam. Ch. 9). Nor does it comport with this patience formerly shown to Shimei (2 Sam. 16:5-13). We can not explain these charges of hatred upon any other grounds than that of an old man in his dotage. He is "no longer his manful self."

Psalms. While the time covered by the collection of the Psalms is more than a thousand years, reaching from the time of Moses to the period of the exile, it is probably best to study them in this period. The majority of them are ascribed to David and the whole collection early became known as the Psalms of David. Reference should be made to The Bible Book By Book for an introduction to their study.

The Lessons of the Period. (1) Divine appointment to a great task does not guarantee one against falling into evil. (2) Luxury and the indulgence of the appetites tend to degradation. (3) The personal forgiveness of sin does not remove its evil consequences. (4) Our sins are often as harmful to others and even more so than to ourselves. (5) Righteousness exalteth a nation. (6) God controls the issues of wars.

For Study and Discussion. (1) The location of the several nations conquered by David and how the victories were won, especially the capture of Jebus. (2) David's plan to build the Temple and God's message to him II Sam. Ch. 11. Point out the different elements in it. (3) Absolom's conspiracy and final defeat, II Sam. Chs. 15 and 18. (4) The death of the child of Uriah's wife, II Sam. Ch. 12. (5) The different times David showed kindness to his enemies, II Sam. 9, 10, 16, and 19. Learn the details of each case. (6) The organization of his kingdom, II Sam. 8:16-18, 15:37, 16:16, 20:23-26; I Chron. 27:33. (7) Tie rebellion of Sheba, II Sam. 20:1-22. (8) The story of Adonijah, I K. Ch. 1. (9) List David's last commands to Solomon, I K. 2:1-9. (10) Nathan's parable to David, II Sam. 12:1-9, 13-15. (11) The greatest fault of Absalom, of Joab. (12) Joab, the avenger, II Sam. 2:17-32, 3:22-30, 18:9-15, 20:4-10.

Chapter XII

Solomon's Reign.

I K. Chs. 1-12; II Chron. Chs.1-9.

The Riddle of Solomon's Character. Few Biblical characters manifested such contradictory elements of character. Early in life he manifested an earnest, conscientious and religious spirit. He was prayerful and sought above all else wisdom and that for the good reason that he might be able to rule well. He built the temple and thereby magnified the worship of Jehovah.

His prayer at the dedication of this temple were not only humble and fervent but were expressive of the very highest loyalty to Jehovah as the one supreme God and to all the high purposes of the divine will in Israel. But in spite of all this he put upon the people such heavy burdens of taxation as to crush them. He trampled under foot the democratic ideals of the nation and adopted the policy of oriental despots which tended to make free-born citizens mere slaves of the king. He lived a life of the basest sort of self-indulgence. He depended upon foreign alliances rather than upon Jehovah to save his nation. He married many strange wives and through them was led to establish in Israel the worship of strange Gods. I K. 11:1-8. On the whole his reign was such as to undo what had been accomplished by David and proved disastrous. Although counted the wisest he proved to be in many ways the most foolish king that ever ruled over Israel.

His Policies. As a ruler it is easy to think of his policies under three heads, (1) His home policy. This was one of absolution. He became a despot and robbed the people of their freedom and put them under a yoke of oppression by imposing upon them heavy burdens of tax that he might carry out his unholy plans for selfish indulgence. (2) His foreign policy. This was a policy of diplomacy. By means of intermarriage, by the establishment of commercial relations and by the adoption of the customs and religions of other nations he bound them in friendly alliance. (3) His religious policy. This was a policy of

60

concentration. He built die temple and, through the splendor of its worship, tried to concentrate all worship upon Mount Moriah. This desire may also have contributed to his erection of altars to foreign deities.

Solomon's Building Enterprise. The greatest of all his building accomplishments was the temple. It is almost impossible to conceive of its magnificence. According to the most modern computation the precious materials, such as gold with which it was embellished, amounted to something like six hundred million dollars. Next in importance was his palace, which in size and time of construction surpassed that of the temple. This palace consisted of several halls, the chief of which were: The Forest of Lebanon, the Hall of Pillars, and the Hall of Judgment. Near the palace was the residence of the king himself and his Egyptian Queen-a house that would compare well with the royal palaces of her native land. Indeed all Moriah and the ground about its base were covered with immense structures.

Besides the temple, palace and other great buildings at the capitol, Solomon undertook various other great building enterprises. He built many great cities not only in the territory of ancient Palestine but in his now extended empire. The most famous of these were Tadmor or Palmyra and Baalath, or Baalbic. The former built at an oasis of the Syrian desert seems to have been a sort of trade emporium for the traders of Syria and the Euphrates to exchange wares with the merchants of Egypt. The latter was near Lebanon and was chiefly notable for its temple of the sun which was one of the finest edifices of Syria.

It would be difficult to put too high a value upon the influence wrought by these vast building enterprises. It can hardly be doubted that the building of the temple was the most important single event of the period of the United Kingdom. From this time on Israel ceased to look back to Sinai and regard Jerusalem as the dwelling place of Jehovah. Its priesthood and services became the support of all the coming kings. The prophets proclaimed their immortal messages from its sacred precincts and through it was nurtured the pure religion of Jehovah.

Solomon's Writings. During this period as in the previous one literary culture made a great advance. Solomon, like David his father, possessed extraordinary literary gifts and as a writer had large influence. Three books of the Scripture are ascribed to him. (1) The Book of Proverbs. There is no reason to believe, however, that he wrote all of them. It is a collection of proverbs or rather several collections. Some were written by Solomon, collected by him from the wise sayings of others and still others were added collections of later times. (2) Ecclesiastes. The purpose of this book seems to be to show the result of successful worldliness and self-gratification compared with a life of godliness. It is intended to show that the realization of all one's aim and hopes and aspirations in the matters of wealth, pleasure and honor will not bring satisfaction to the heart. (3) The Song of Solomon. To the Jews of that time this book set forth the whole of the history of Israel; to the Christian it sets forth the fullness of love that unites the believer and his Savior as bride and bridegroom; to all the world it is a call to cast out those unworthy ideals and monstrous practices that threaten to undermine society and the home.

Nations Surrounding Israel. The life of any people is always influenced by the nations around them. During this period Israel had intercourse with many other nations. (1) Phoenicia. This commercial people, through Hiram of Tyre, one of its kings, supplied the cedar wood and the skilled laborers who made possible the building of the temple. (2) Egypt. Solomon married a daughter of Pharoah and carried on with Egypt an extensive commerce and for his wife's sake no doubt introduced the worship of Egyptian gods. (3) Assyria. This country as well as Egypt had lost much of her former power and was not in a position to antagonize Solomon. (4) Among the other nations with which Solomon had dealings may be mentioned Sheba, thought to be in the most southern part of Arabia, Ophir and Tarshish, and from the nature of articles purchased and the three years required for the voyage he is thought to have sent trading vessels to India.

Evidences of National Decay. From the brief history of this period given us by the biblical writers it is evident that the nation began to disintegrate before the death of Solomon. Among the more apparent signs of decay were several revolts: (1) that of Hadad the Edomite, who threw off the Hebrew part of Edom independently: (2) that of Adad, the Midianite, who defiled the authority of Solomon; (3) that of Rezon, the Aramean, who revolted and became master of Damascus around which grew up an important kingdom; (4) that of Jeroboam, an Ephraimite, who was an officer of Solomon at Jerusalem and while unsuccessful showed the existence of a deep-seated discontent in Jerusalem itself. It is significant that the prophet Ahijah of Shiloh encouraged Jeroboam by telling him that, on account of the idolatry fostered by Solomon, ten tribes would be removed from Solomon's son and committed to him. This indicates that the prophets saw that disunion alone would preserve the liberties and pure religion of Israel.

Lessons of the Period. (1) All national methods bring disaster if God is left out of account. (2) Material progress is absolutely of no value without a spiritual life. (3) National prosperity always endangers the nation. (4) The wisest and best of men may go wrong, if they subject themselves to evil influences. (5) Temples or houses of worship are of value in giving dignity to faith and in preserving the spirit of worship. (6) If the common people feel that they are unjustly treated nothing will prevent the disintegration of the nation. (7) Religion that does not issue in proper ethics will suffer at the hands of true ethics. (8) The security of society depends upon simple justice.

For Study and Discussion. (1) The several incidents attending Solomon's accession to the throne, I K. Chs. 1-2. (2) David's last charge to Solomon, I K. Ch. 3; 4:29:34. (4) [sic] Solomon's temple: (a) Its size and plan; (b) Its equipment; (c) Its dedication. (5) Solomon's prayer at the dedication of the temple, I K. Ch. 8: II Chron. Ch. 6. Look for a revelation of his character, religious spirit and conception of God. (6) Solomon's sins, I K. Ch. 11. (7) Solomon's treatment of his foes I K, 2:19-46. (8). What Solomon did to stimulate trade, I K. 9:26-10:13; 10:22-29. (9) Statements in Ecclesiastes that point to Solomon as author or to experiences he had. (10) Statements in Song of Solomon that throw light upon the times or seem to refer to Solomon and his experiences.

Chapter XIII

The Divided Kingdom.

1 King, 12-2 K. 17. 2 Chron. 10-38.

The Division of the Kingdom. Several things must be set down as contributory causes of the division of the nation. (1) There was an old jealousy between the tribes of the north and south reaching as far back as the time of the Judges. The very difference in the northern and southern territories and their products tended to keep alive a rivalry between the tribes occupying them. (2) During the time of Solomon the people had turned away from Jehovah and engaged in the idolatrous worship of other gods, especially those of the Zidonians, Moabites and Ahijah, the prophet, had foretold the division (1 K. 11:29-39). This weakening of the people's faithfulness to God gave place for the manifestations of their former jealousy. (3) Solomon had put upon the people heavy burdens of taxation and of forced labor, which were fast taking away the people's liberties and reducing them to serfdom. This policy inflamed the jealousy of the northern tribes into a bitter discontent. They would rebel rather than submit to the loss of their liberty which to them meant also disloyalty to God. (4) The ambition of Jeroboam, of the tribe of Ephraim, a valiant officer of Solomon, no doubt led him to stir up the ten tribes to revolt. Ahijah, the prophet, had made known to him that, upon the death of Solomon, he should become the head of these tribes. (5) The final and immediate cause was the foolish course of Rehoboam. He went to Shechem to be accepted as king by the northern tribes. They demanded that he should relieve them of the heavy burdens laid on them by Solomon. The older and more experienced men counseled him to grant their request, but he heeded the advice of the young men, who were ignorant of conditions, and answered them with a threat of even severer burdens. Incensed by this foolish threat, the ten tribes revolted and enthroned Jeroboam as their king and the division of the empire was accomplished. This was the turning point of the nation. It was the undoing of all that had been accomplished by the three kings that had proceeded.

Comparison of the Two Kingdoms. Each kingdom had its advantages and its disadvantages. (1) The northern kingdom, from the material point of view, was far superior to the southern. It had a larger and more fertile country. It had three times as many people and a much better military equipment. Ramah, Bether and Gilgal with their sites of their schools of the prophets were all in their borders. Their country was also the scene of greatest prophetic activity and their cause was just. But the kings were inferior and wicked. Not a single one of the nineteen kings were godly. They established idolatrous and abominable worship as a religion of the king. This idolatry counterbalanced all the material advantages. (2) The Southern Kingdom was far superior from a spiritual point of view. It possessed the religious capital of the nation with the temple as a center of Jehovah worship. True it had only one third as many people, one half as much territory and that less fertile, and an inferior military equipment, but its superior spiritual power and its superior line of kings made it last 135 years longer than the northern kingdom.

The Kings of the Northern Kingdom.

1. Jeroboam, 1 K. 12:20-14:20. Reigned 22 years and died.
2. Nadab, 1 K. 15:25-27. Reigned 2 years and was slain.
3. Baasha, 1 K. 15;27-16:6. Reigned 24 years and died.
4. Elah, 1 K. 16;6-10. Reigned 2 years and was slain.
5. Zimri, 1 K. 18:11-20. Reigned 7 days and suicided.
6. Omri, 1 K. 16:31-28. Reigned 12 years and died.
7. Ahab, 1 K. 16:29-22:40. Reigned 22 years and was slain in battle.
8. Ahaziah, 1 K. 22:51-2 K. 1:18. Reigned 2 years and died from an accident.
9. Jehoram, 2 K. 3:1-9:24. Reigned 12 years and was slain.
10. Jehu, 2 K. 9:1-10:36. Reigned 28 years and died.
11. Jehoahaz, 2 K. 13:1-9. Reigned 17 years and died.
12. Jehoash, 2 K. 13:10-14:16. Reigned 16 years and died.
13. Jeroboam II, 2 K. 14:23-29. Reigned 41 years and died.
14. Zechariah, 2 K. 15:8-10. Reigned 6 months and was slain.
15. Shallum, 2 K. 15:13-14. Reigned 1 month and was slain.
16. Menahem, 2 K. 15:14-22. Reigned 10 years and died.

17. Pekahian, 2 K. 15:23-26. Reigned 2 years and was slain.

18. Pekah, 2 K. 15:27-16:9. Reigned 20 years and was slain.

19. Hoshea, 2 K. 17:1-6. Reigned 9 years and put in prison.

The Kings of Judah.

1. Rehoboam, 1 K. 12:21-24; 14:21-31; 2 Chron. 11:1-12:16. Reigned 17 years and died.

2. Abijah, 1 K. 15:1-8; 2 Chron. 13:1-22. Reigned 3 years and died.

3. Asa, 1 K. 15:9-24; 2 Chron. 14:1-16:14. Reigned 41 years and died.

4. Jehoshaphat, 1 K. 13:24; 23:41-50; 2 K. 3:1-27; 2 Chron. 17:1-21:1 Reigned 25 years and died.

5. Jeboram, 2 K. 8:16-24; 2 Chron. 21:1-20. Reigned 8. years and died.

6. Ahaziah, 2 K. 8:25-29; 9:27-29; 2 Chron. 22:1-9. Reigned 1 year and was killed by order of Jehu.

7. Athaliah, 2 K. 11:1-21:2; 2 Chron, 22;10-23:6. Reigned 6 years and was slain when Joash became king.

8. Joash, 2 K. 11:3-12:21; 2 Chron. 24:1-27. Reigned 40 years and was slain.

9. Amaziah, 2 K. 14:1-20; 2 Chron. 25:1-28. Reigned 29 years and was slain.

10. Uzziah or Azariah, 2 K. 14:21-25; 2 Chron. 28:1-23. Reigned 52 years and died.

11. Jotham, 2 K. 15:32-36; 2 Chron. 27:1-9. Reigned IB years and died.

12. Ahaz, 2 K. 16:1-30: 2 Chron. 28:1-27. Reigned IS years and died.

Important Events in the History of Israel. The following are perhaps the most important events in the history of tie northern kingdom during this period. (1) The establishment of idol worship at Dan and Bethel. (2) The removal of the Capital, by Omri, from Tirzah to the hill site of Samaria. (3) The wicked reign of Ahab, who introduced Baal worship into Israel. (4) The reformations of Jehu, who swept Baal worship from the land and overthrew the hated dynasty of Omri. (5) The successful reign of Jeroboam II, who brought the nation back to a state of prosperity that resembled the time of David and Solomon. (6) The activity of the prophets during the entire period. This activity is seen in the important place given (1 K. 17-2 K. 13) to the work of Elijah and Elisha; in the prophecy of Jonah, Amos and Hosea, who prophesied in the time of the reign of Jereboam II, and in part in the reign of Micah who preached during the reign of Hoshea. (7) The conquest of Israel by the Assyrians which came as the result of forty years of constant decline following the death of Jeroboam II. After this Israel disappears from history. She had sinned away her opportunity.

Principal Events In the History of Judah. The following are the principal events of the history of Judah from the division of the kingdom until the captivity of Israel. (1) The foolish answer of Rehoboam to the ten tribes which led to their revolt and the continual enmity of the northern and southern kingdoms that followed. (2) The invasion of Judah by Shishak of Egypt, who greatly weakened the nation. (3) The reign of Jehoshaphat whose judicial, military and educational or religious reforms introduce a new and good day in Judah and whose unhappy alliance with Ahab, led his son, who followed him as king to introduce idolatry into Judah, with all the evil of the reign of Jehoram, Ahaziah and Athaliah. (4) The prosperous reign of Uzziah, who was contemporary with Jeroboam II of Israel. (5) The Apostasy under Ahaz, who encouraged Baal worship and practiced great cruelty even on the members of his own family. The prophet Isaiah (chs. 7-9) appeals to Ahaz and to the people to return to Jehovah.

The Relation between the Two Kingdoms. The bearing of the two kingdoms toward each other during this period was constantly changing. (1) There was almost constant war for about sixty years. During this time the kings of Judah cherished the hope that they would regain their control over the ten tribes. (2) There was a period of close alliance. This alliance was sealed by an intermarriage between the families of Ahab, king of Israel and Jehoshaphat, king of Judah. The purpose seems to have been that they might better resist the encroaching power of Assyria. (3) There was a fresh manifestation of hatred. Jehu is enthroned in Israel and destroys the house of Ahab. This shatters the alliance between the two nations and causes a breach that is never healed. The northern kingdom becomes more and more idolatrous, suffers at the hands of the Syrians and is finally carried captive by the Assyrians in 722 B. C.

The Messages of the Prophets of this Period. It is not within the purpose of this study to raise any of the questions of criticism concerning these books. Nor is there time to summarize the contents or teachings of nay or all of them. The prophets of this period are Jonah, Amos and Hosea, and the prophecy of each should be read following the outline given in the author's The Bible Book by Book.

Lessons of the Period. (1) Jehovah rules not only in Israel but over all peoples. (2) Each nation is responsible to God according to its opportunity and enlightenment. (3) God judges people according to their acts, not according to religious creeds or ceremonies. (4)Though a merciful God, Jehovah will and must finally punish willful and continuous evil doers. (5) Sin is infidelity to God and brings pain to his heart. (6) All punishment is administered to the end that the sinful may repent and be forgiven. (7) Jehovah loves men and demands that they love him in return. (8) Repentance is the only way of escape from doom. (9) God seeks to save men and nations from the sins that are to destroy them.

For Study and Discussion. (1) The events leading to the division of the kingdom. (2) The story of each king in each nation, (a) How he came to the throne, (b) The chief acts of his reign, (c) The character of the king himself, (d) The length of his reign, (e) His enemies and his friends, (f) How his reign ended. (3) The story of Ahab. (4) The story of Elijah. (5) The story of Elisha. (6) The miracles of the period. (7) The different enemies with which the tribes were surrounded and the trouble they had with each. (8) Jonah and his service. (9) The evidence of wealth and luxury of the time. (10) The sins of cruelty and injustice in society and government.

Chapter XIV

The Kingdom of Judah.

II K. 18-25; II Chron. 28-36.

Note: This period covers the time from the fail of Israel to the fall of Judah. It begins in the sixth year of the reign of Hezekiah, whose name is given as the first king of the period since most of his reign was in this instead of the former period.

The Kings of this Period.

13. Hezekiah, 2 K. 18:1-20-21; 2 Chron. 29:1-32:33. Reigned 29 years and died.

14. Manasseh, 2 K. 21:1-18; 2 Chron. 33:1-20. Reigned 55 year and died.

15. Amon, 2 K. 21:19-26; 2 Chron. 33:20-25. Reigned 2 years and was slain by a conspiracy of his servants.

16. Josiah, 2 K. 22:1-23; 2 Chron. 34:1-33:27. Reigned 31 years and was killed in battle.

17. Jehoahaz. 2 K. 23:30-34; 2 Chron. 36:1-4. Reigned 3 months and was dethroned and carried into Egypt where he died.

18. Jehoiakim, 2 K. 23:34-24:6; 2 Chron. 36:4-8. Reigned 11 years and died.

19. Jehoiachin. 2 K. 24:6-16; 2 Chron. 36:9-10. Reigned 3 months and was carried captive to Egypt.

20. Zedekiah. 2 K. 24:17-25; 2 Chron. 36:11-21. Reigned 11 years and carried captive into Egypt.

The Principal Events of the Period. Among the more important events of this period the following should be noticed. (1) The reforms of Hezekiah who attempted to restore the whole Mosaic order. (2) The invasion of Judah by Sennacherib, king of Assyria who at first humiliated Hezekiah, but later, was destroyed by divine intervention and Jerusalem saved. (3) The wicked reign of Manasseh, who sought to destroy all true worship and established idolatrous worship in its stead. (4) His captivity in Babylon and release and attempted reform. (5) The good reign of Josiah, who destroyed the altars of idolatry, repaired the temple and caused the book of the law to be read-all of which resulted in a very thorough-going revival of true worship. (6) The conflicts with their enemies which finally resulted in the downfall of Jerusalem and the captivity of the people. This captivity was completely accomplished through three invasions of the hosts of Nebuchadnezzar, (a) In the reign of Jehoiakim at which time he carried away captive Daniel and his friends; (b) In the reign of Jehoiachin or Jeconiah, when he carried to Babylon the treasures of Jerusalem and the skilled workmen as well as the officers of the court; (c) In the reign of Zedekiah, when the city and temple and walls and principal houses were destroyed and large numbers carried into captivity.

The Prophets of the Period and Their Messages. Of all the periods this is signalized by the greatest prophetic activity. There was constant need both on the part of the king and on the part of the people for the warnings and rebukes of the people. Some prophets delivered part of their message in one period and the rest in another. No doubt Isaiah and Micah did part of their service during the former period and Jeremiah performed a part of his in the next. But they are all put down here because this is the period of their greatest activity. The other prophets of the period are Joel, Nahum, Zephaniah, Habakkuk and Obadiah. The messages of these prophets should be carefully read following outlines given in The Bible Book by Book.

The Teachings of the Prophets. It is difficult to put down in brief form the various teachings announced and implied in the writings of the prophets. Their sermons covered a wide range of subjects, religious, political, commercial and social. They touch upon matters that are national and also those that are personal. The following may be regarded as among their most important teachings. (1) That Jehovah is a moral being-holy, just, wise and good. (2) That Jehovah was the God not only of Judah and of Israel but off all nations. (3) That no man, no set of men and no nation can thwart the plans of God. (4) That God's judgments were certain to overtake the sinful. (5) That religion was not separate from life, but the very central factor of it-that religion and ethics are so blended that "to act justly, to love mercy and to walk humbly before his God" is shown to be man's whole duty. (6) That religion is a personal spiritual relation between God and man. This is especially the contribution of Jeremiah and lays the foundation for all true faith and is a basal principle of our Christianity.

The False Prophets, Through all the history of Israel false prophets were a source of great trouble. Among those of earlier times may be noted: (1) An old prophet of Bethel, 1 K. 13:11. (2) 400 prophets with a lying spirit, 1 K. 22:6-8. 22-23. (3) 450 prophets of Baal, 1 K. 18:19, 22, 40. (4) 400 prophets of Asherah. 1 K. 18:19. A study of these will show that some are idolatrous prophets and others are perverted worshipers of Jehovah, who did not really prophesy at all. Some were no doubt deliberate deceivers of the people while others were perhaps self-deceived.

During the years immediately preceding the Babylonian captivity false prophets played a prominent role and their pernicious influence upon Judah's history can hardly be overestimated. They lured the people to their ruin and undermined the influence of the true prophets. Isaiah talks about the prophet that teaches lies (Is. 9:15). Jeremiah talks of prophets of lies, who prophesy, not having been sent of Jehovah (Jer. 14:13-15; 23:21-22). Micah tells of the prophets who make the people err (Mi. 3:5). Jeremiah was openly opposed by Hananiah (Jer. Ch. 28). These prophets destroyed confidence in the message of true prophets and brought about a time when the voice of these messengers of God ceased to be heard in Israel.

The Great Religious Revivals of this Period. The whole history of the kingdom of Judah is marked by periods of religious decline and revival. The most striking of these are indicated by the following outline. (1) A decline under the reign of Rehoboam. (2) A revival begun under Asa and made complete under the reign of Jehoshaphat; (3) A decline begun in the reign of Jehoram and continued until the reign of Ahaz where the lowest spiritual state was reached. (4) A new revival under Hezekiah, who introduced sweeping social and religious changes. (5) A decline under Manasseh who reared images to Baal, defiled the temple and overthrew the good work of his father Hezekiah. (6) A revival under Josiah, grandson of Manasseh, whose piety began to manifest itself at the age of sixteen. He began his reforms at the age of twenty and spent six years in hewing down the altars and images of idolatry. The temple was repaired, the law found and enjoined upon the people and the Passover celebrated. (7) A final decline that carried Judah on downward until her glory was destroyed and she was led away into Babylon as captive.

The study of these successive efforts at returning to the true worship of Jehovah and their quick collapse indicate that the kindlings of spiritual life which they seem to manifest were not real spiritual revivals. Many people did no doubt turn in truth to God. but the rapidity with which each effort was followed by a return to deeper depths of immorality, such as those indicated by Amos 5:16, 7:17, 8:6; Is. 1:23, 10:1; and Hos. 9:15 give evidence of the abounding wickedness of the period.

The Wealth and Luxury. There is much in the discourses to indicate that wealth abounded and that kings and other influential men lived in luxury. The upper classes indulged in all the follies of the idle rich and showed the usual heartlessness toward the poor. The following list of scriptures will indicate some of the things which they possessed and which they did: Amos 5:11, 3:15, 6:4; Jer. 22:14; Is. 5:ll-12, 3:18-23, 21:7. To this list the student by comparison and reference can add many others.

Contemporary Nations. No study of this period would be complete without a knowledge of the other nations that influenced this time. Egypt, Assyria, Babylon, Media, Phoenicia, Carthage, Greece and Rome all influenced Judah. From the Bible narratives and from secular history the student should become acquainted with the leading events in the history of this period of each of these nations.

Lessons of the Period. It is most difficult to put down the permanent lessons or teachings of this period. To the teachings of the prophets given above the following are well worth preserving as lessons for our day as well as theirs. (1) All reformation must begin at the house of God and in connection with his worship-witness the reform work of Asa, Jehoshaphat, Joash, Hezekiah and Josiah. (2) Religion must set the standards for the conduct of national affairs. (3) Sin is infidelity to love, or spiritual adultery. It not only breaks law but cruelly wounds love. (4) Sin blinds men to their best interests, turns them against their best friends and issues in their ruin. (5) The political sentiment or the politician that neglects or attacks God, or the national recognition of him is perilous to the nation. (6) The loss of the sense or vision of God leads to "degraded ideals, deadened consciences and defeated purposes."

(7) True love: (a) is not blind to the sins of the one loved; (b) does not try to cover up the faults but tries to turn one from them; (c) does not desert one when calamity comes because of persistence in sin. See the attitude of Jeremiah to Judah before and after the captivity.

For Study and Discussion. (1) Study each of the teachings of the prophets given above: (a) Try to find scripture basis for it; (b) Discuss it as a universal principle. (2) Study each of the scriptures referred to in the discussion above on false prophets: (a) From references collect other passages on the subject; (b) Make a list of their prophecies and tell how to determine whether a prophet is false. (3) From the scriptures given above on wealth and luxury and from others to be pointed out: (a) List the evidences of wealth; (b) Compare the conditions then and now. (4) Following the instructions for study in the paragraph above on contemporaneous nations prepare a list of facts concerning each, especially of matters that affected Judah. (5) Name the kings of this period. Tell (a) how each came into office, (b) how long he reigned, (c) how his career ended, (d) what prophet preached to each and the nature of the prophecy. (6) Hezekiah's sickness, 2 King 20:1-11; 2 Chron. 32;24-26; (7) His song of thanksgiving, Is. 38:10-20. Carefully analyze it. (8) Sennacherib's invasion, 2 K. 18:14-19 end; Is. 14:24-27; 36:1-37:10; 2 Chron. 32:1-23. (a) The object of the expedition; (b) The conference with Hezekiah; (c) The outcome. (9) Josiah's reformations. (10) The three invasions of Nebuchadnezzar.

Chapter XV

The Captivity of Judah.

Eze., Dan., Lam.

The Ten Tribes Lost. After the fall of Samaria we hear but little of the ten tribes. They were carried off into the regions of Ninevah by the Assyrians. All effort to locate them has failed and no doubt will fail. Sargon, in an inscription found at Ninevah, said that he carried away into captivity 27,290. These were perhaps leaders of Israel whom he thought might lead a revolt. He sent others back to take their place and the Israelites seemed to have mingled with the races about them and to have lost their identity. No doubt some of them as individuals were faithful to the worship of Jehovah and may have found their way back to Palestine under the leadership of Ezra and Nehemiah. But it was different with Judah who all the time kept true to her ideals and looked for the return that had been prophesied. This hope was realized through the work of Ezra and Nehemiah following the decree of Cyrus.

Judah Led into Captivity. The captivity of Judah was accomplished by three distinct invasions of the Babylonians and covered a period of twenty years. (1) The first invasion and captivity. This was in 607 B.C., at which time Daniel and his friends along with others were carried into captivity, 2 K. 24:1, Jer. 25:1, Dan. 1:1-7. (2) The second invasion and captivity. This was 597 B.C., at which time king Jehoiakim and 10.000 of the people were carried into captivity. Among these were Ezekiel and one of the ancestors of Mordicai, the cousin of Esther, 2 K. 24:10-16; Eze. 1:1-2; Est. 2:5-6. (3) The third invasion and captivity. In 587 B.C. Jerusalem was conquered and its walls and palaces as well as the temple were destroyed and the inhabitants carried away into exile, 2 K. 24:18; 24:1-27; 2 Chron. 36:11-21; Jer. 52:1-11. This is the end of the southern kingdom.

The Period of the Captivity. Jeremiah predicts that the captivity will last seventy years (Jer. 25:12; 29:10; see 2 Chron. 36:21; Dan. 9:2: Zech. 7:6). There are two ways of adjusting the dates to fulfill this prediction,

74

(1) From the first invasion and the carrying into captivity of Daniel and others, 607 B. C. to 537 B. C., when the first company returned under Zerubbabel. (2) From the final fall of Jerusalem. 587 B. C. to the completion of the renewed temple and its dedication, 517 B. C. Either satisfies the scripture. In history it is customary to speak of this exile as covering only the fifty years from 587 B. C. when Jerusalem was destroyed and the last company carried away to 537 B. C. when the first company returned under Zerubbabel.

The Fugitives in Egypt. When Jerusalem fell the king of Babylon allowed many of the poorer people to remain in Palestine and Jedediah, a grandson of Josiah, was appointed to rule over them. 2 K. 25:22. His career was a very useful one, but through jealousy he was soon murdered, 2 K. 25:25. This led the people to fear lest Nebuchadnezzar would avenge his death, whereupon they fled into Egypt 2 K. 25:26. Jeremiah attempted to keep them from going to Egypt (Jer. 42:9-22.) but, when he failed, he went along with them and shared their destiny, Jer. 43:6-7. They settled at Tahpanhee (Jer. 44:1), a frontier town where many foreigners lived under the protection of Egypt. They seem to have built a temple there and did much to retain their racial ideals. Jeremiah seems to have continued his faithful prophecies and the people seem to have continued as faithfully to reject his counsel. We do not know how he ended his career but Jewish tradition says he was put to death by his own people.

The Exiles in Babylon. The state of the exiles in Babylon may not be fully known but from the contemporary writers very much may be known. (1) Their home. They were settled in a rich and fertile plain, intersected by many canals. It was on the river, or canal, Chebar (Ez. 1:1.3; 3:15, etc.) which ran southeast from Babylon to Nippur. It was a land of traffic and merchants and fruitful fields (Ez. 17:4-5). They were rather colonists than slaves and enjoyed great freedom and prosperity. (2) Their occupation. By reason of their intellectual and moral superiority the Jews, as they are called from this time forward, would secure rapid advancement. Some of them such as Daniel obtained high position. Others became skilled workmen. Following the advice of Jeremiah (Jer. 29:5), many of them no doubt gave themselves to agriculture and gardening. Probably most of them yielded to the opportunities of the "land of traffic and merchants" mentioned above and engaged in commercial instead of agricultural pursuits. (3) Their government. For a long time they were allowed to control their own affairs as their own laws provided. The elders of the families acted as judges and directed affairs in general. For a while they probably held the power of life and death over their own people, but the capital cases were punished later by authority of Babylon (Jer. 29:22.) (4) Their religion. Here also the information is meager and must be gathered from statements and inferences found in several books. Several things are certain: (a) For the most part they preserved their genealogies, thus making possible the identity of the Messiah as well as their proper place in worship when they were restored; (b) They gave up all idolatry and were never again led into its evil practices as they had been wont to do before. Indeed, there are, even to the present day, no idolatrous Jews; (c) They gave up the elaborate ceremonials and the public and private sacrifices and the great festivals. In their stead prayer and fasting and Sabbath observances constituted the main part of their religious life. The observance of the Sabbath became a ceremony and was robbed of its simple divine purpose; (d) They assembled the people together on the Sabbath for the purpose of prayer and the reading of the scripture. This custom probably formed the basis for synagogue worship so influential later; (e) All this private devotion and prayer such as was seen in the thrice-a-day worship of Daniel was opening the way for a purer and more spiritual religion; (f) The Canon was greatly enlarged and new spiritual teachings were announced or new light thrown on old teachings. The prophesies of Daniel and Ezekiel with many psalms were added. The book of Lamentations and chapters 40-44 of Jeremiah were also the products of this date but refer especially to the conditions of those in Egypt.

The Prophets of the Exile. This period is calculated to bring great discouragement to the Jews. They so far failed of their expectations that there is danger that they will give up their proper regard for Jehovah. They have great need that some one tell them the significance of their suffering and point out for them some word of hope for the future. This service was rendered by the prophets. There was great activity on the part of false prophets (Jer. 39:4-8, 21-23; Ez. 13:1-7, 14:8-10), but they were blessed by the following true prophets: (1) Ezekiel. These prophecies began by recounting the incidents of the prophet's call and the incidents between the first and the second captivities; they then denounce those nations that had part in the destruction of Jerusalem and those that had been bitter and oppressive in their dealings with Israel and Judah; they close with messages of comfort and cheer for the exiled people; (2) Daniel. (3) Lamentations. Besides a portion of the book of Jeremiah and probably of Isaiah which, as suggested above, belongs to this period, the book of Lamentations, written while in exile in Egypt, should be placed here. All three of these books should be read by following the outline given in The Bible Book by Book.

The Benefits of the Captivity, Dr. Burroughs gives as benefits that the Jews derived from the captivity the following four things: (1) the destruction of idolatry; (2) the rise of the synagogue; (3) a deepened respect for the law of Moses; (4) a longing for the Messiah. To these might be added or emphasized as being included in them: (1) a vital sense of repentance was created; (2) the change from the national, festal and ceremonial worship to a spiritual and individual religion; (3) a belief that Israel had been chosen and trained in order that through her Jehovah might bless the whole world.

Lessons of the Period. The experiences of Judah as recorded in this period bring us several important truths. (1) That sin will tear down both men and nations. (2) Men are responsible and suffer for their own sins but not for the sins of others, Ez. 18:2-3; 33:10-11. (3) God controls all circumstances toward the ultimate accomplishment of his purposes. (4) He makes free use of all "world rulers as his tools to execute his will" (5) God sets up and destroys nations. (6) God cares for his people and overrules all for their good. See Dan., etc. (7) One can live right in spite of one's surroundings (see Daniel) and such living will lead men to know God. (8) Evil grows more and more determined while good grows more and more distinct and hence the question "Is the world growing better?" (9) God rejoices in the opportunity to forgive his erring people and in restoring them again into his partnership.

For Study and Discussion, (1) When, to whom and by whom the exile was predicted: (a) 2 K. 20:17-18; (b) 2 K. 21:10-16; (c) 2 K. 22:16-17, Dt. 28:25, 52-68; (d) Jer. 25:9-11; (e) Jer. 34:2-3; (f) Mic. 3:12; (g) Zeph. 1:2-6. (2) The different classes of exiles: (a) Those in favor with the court, Dan. 1:19-21, 2:45-49; (b) Common laborers-lower classes, Jer. ch. 29, Eze. ch. 13; (c) Pretentious prophets, Eze. ch. 13, Jer. ch. 29.

(3) The social condition of the exiles, 2 K. 25:27; Dan. 1:19-21; Is. 60:1; Jer. 29:4-7, Esth., and passages in Eze. (4) The details of each of the three invasions and the captivities as outlined above. See scriptures. (5) The exiles in Egypt: (a) Who they were, (b) How they fared. (6) The activity and influence of false prophets of this age. (7) The story of Nebuchadnezzar's dreams and their interpretation: (a) the image dream, (b) the tree dream. (8) The stories of (a) The fiery furnace; (b) of the lion's den. (9) The feast of Belshazzar. (10) The visions of Daniel 7:1-14, 8:1-12, 10:4-6. (11) The four beasts of Daniel and their significance. (12) The oracles against foreign nations, Eze. chs. 25-32. (13) The benefits mentioned above. (14) The lessons mentioned above. Find scripture basis for them.

Chapter XVI

The Restoration.

Ezra, Neh., Esth., Hag., Zech.

Scripture Analysis. The books of Ezra and Nehemiah furnish the outline of the period and its achievements. The two books were formerly counted one book and a continuous outline of the two is best suited to the proper emphasis of the various events of the period. The following outline will appear simple and yet sufficient for our purpose. (1) The rebuilding of the temple (Ezra, chs. 1-6). (2) The reforms of Ezra (Ezra, chs. 7-10). (3) The rebuilding of the walls (Neh. chs. 1-7). (4) The covenant to keep the law (Neh. chs. 8-10). (5) The inhabitants of Jerusalem (Neh. 11:1-12:26). (6) The dedication of the wall and the reform of Nehemiah (Neh. 12:27-13-end).

Predictions of the Return. The return from captivity had been prophesied long before the fall of Jerusalem. Several prophets had foretold the captivity and in connection with it had told of the destruction of Babylon and Judah's restoration. Even the length of their stay in exile was announced. While they were in exile they were constantly encouraged by the promised return foretold to them by Ezekiel, Jeremiah and others. (1) Restoration at the end of seventy years is predicted. (Jer. 25:12; 29:10; Dan. 9:2). (2) Other Scriptures that foretell the overthrow of Babylon or the return to Jerusalem or both may be found in Is. chs. 13, 14, 21, 44-47; Jer. 28:4-11; chs. 50-52; Ez. ch. 27, etc.

The Rise of Persian Power. This was a period of world change. Great empires in rapid succession fell under the power of new and rising kingdoms. (1) The Assyrian Empire, which superseded the Chaldean Empire about 1500 B. C., and now loomed so large in the eyes of the world, fell, when the combined forces of the Medes and Babylonians captured Ninevah her capital (B. C. 607) and was numbered among the dead nations. (2) The Babylonian Empire rose to supremacy and was the dominating power when Judah went into captivity. She was the most splendid kingdom the world had ever seen. (3) The Persian power conquered Media and the greater part of Assyria and the Medo-Persian Empire under Cyrus conquered Babylon and held almost universal sway at the time of the restoration.

The Decree of Cyrus. It is now about 150 years since Isaiah in his prophesies called Cyrus by name and predicted that he should restore God's captive people to their own land and now in fulfillment of that prophecy God stirred up the spirit of Cyrus and caused him to issue a proclamation for the return of the Jews and the rebuilding of the temple. He gave orders that his people should give the Jews silver, gold and beasts. He also restored to them the vessels of the house of the Lord (Ezra. 1:1-3) and instructed the governors along the way to assist him.

Three Expeditions to Jerusalem. The return from Babylon covered a long period of time and consisted of three separate detachments under as many different leaders. There were important intervening events and contributory causes. (1) The first colony to return was under Zerubhabel (536 B. C.) and consisted of about fifty thousand. Ezra chs. 1-6. We have given us the records of activities of this colony for a period of about twenty-one years, during which time the temple was rebuilt and dedicated. Much opposition was encountered in the matter of rebuilding the temple and the work was finally stopped. It is here that Haggai and Zechariah delivered their stirring prophesies which together with the influence of Jerubbabel and Jeshua, the priest, stimulated the people to renew their building operations and complete the temple (B. C. 515). In the course of history, Haggai and Zechariah would come in between the fourth and fifth chapters of Ezra. (2) The second colony returned to Jerusalem under the leadership of Ezra (Ezra chs. 7-10) and consisted of about 1800 males with their families. There is here a lapse of about fifty-seven years from the completion and dedication of the temple to the time of Ezra's going to Jerusalem-the last thirty years of the reign of Darius, the twenty years of the reign of Xerxes and seven years of the reign of Artaxerxes. Ezra obtained permission from Artaxerxes to return and also letters of instruction to the rulers to give him assistance. He was a scribe of the law of Moses and his mission was primarily a religious one. He was a descendant from the house of Aaron and as such he assumed the office of priest when he reached Jerusalem. Upon his arrival he found that the first colony had fallen into gross immoralities and into unsound religious practices. He rebuke He rebuke all these sins and brought about a great reform. It is not certain that he remained in Jerusalem. His leave from the king may have been only temporary and he may have gone back to Babylon and returned again to Jerusalem in the time of Nehemiah. (3) The third colony was led to Jerusalem by Nehemiah (the book of Nehemiah). The number returning is not given. Nehemiah was the cupbearer to the Persian king and upon hearing of the distress of his people at Jerusalem secured permission from him to go to Jerusalem as the governor. In spite of very determined opposition he was enabled to repair the wall of the city and dedicate it with great ceremony (Neh. chs. 6 and 12). Nehemiah is counted as one of the greatest reformers. He corrected many abuses such as those of usury and restored the national life of the Jews based upon the written law. Together with Ezra he restored the priests to their positions and renewed the temple worship. He went back to the Persian court where he remained several years and then returned to Jerusalem and continued his reforms. This ends the Old Testament history.

The Prophecy of Hagai and Zechariah. The task of these prophets was the same and was by no means an easy one. The work of rebuilding the temple, which had been begun when Jerubbabel and his colony came to Jerusalem, had been stopped by the opposition which they met. Along with this laxity of effort to build the temple the Jews were busy building houses for themselves (1:4) and had become very negligent of all duty. They had begun to despair of seeing their people and the beloved city and temple restored to the glory pictured by the prophets and were rapidly becoming reconciled to the situation. These two prophets succeeded in arousing interest and confidence in the people and through their appeals secured the finishing of the temple.

The Prophecy of Malachi. This prophecy condemns the same sins as those mentioned in the last chapters of Ezra and Nehemiah. He denounced their impure marriages, their lack of personal godliness, their failure to pay tithes and their skepticism. The special occasion for the discourses was the discontent which arose because their expectation of the glorious Messianic Kingdom had not been realized. They had also had unfavorable harvests. It is thought by many that the time of the prophecy is between the first and second visit of Nehemiah to

Jerusalem. The purpose seems to be: (1) to rebuke them for departing from the law; (2) to call them back to Jehovah; (3) to revive the national spirit.

The Story of Esther. King Ahasuerus of the book of Esther is thought to be Xerxes the Great. On this view the events narrated occurred some time before the second colony came to Jerusalem and the story would fall between chapters 6 and 7 of the book of Ezra. The book throws much light on the condition of the Jews in captivity and also upon the social and political conditions existing in the Persian Empire at this period. While the name of God does not occur in the book, his providential care over his people is everywhere manifested. The deliverance of the Jews from death by the intercessions of Esther became the occasion of the establishment of the feast of Purim which ever after commemorated it in Jewish history. These four books should be read following the outline given in The Bible Book by Book.

Synagogues and Synagogue Worship. The emphasis which Ezra gave to the study of the Book of the Law no doubt did much to destroy idolatry and led to a new devotion to the word of God, at least to the letter of the law. This led to the institution or the re-establishment of the Synagogue. There had no doubt been from the early times local gatherings for worship, but the Synagogue worship does not seem to have been in use before the captivity, After the captivity, however, they built many of them, in every direction. They were places of worship where they engaged in reading the law, in exhortation and in prayer. The reading and expounding of the law became a profession, those following this calling being designated "lawyers."

The Significance of the Period, In all the annals of national life there is probably not a more significant sweep of history than that of the Jews during the restoration which covers a little more than ninety years. With the captivity their national life had ceased and now that they are back in their own land they do not seem to make any attempt to reestablish the nation. Stress is now put upon the true worship of God and it is beginning to dawn upon them that the glory of God will be manifested in some higher spiritual sense than had been expected. They had seen the decay of the mightiest material kingdoms, while spiritual Israel lived on, and were seeing how God and his cause and those whom he saves can not die. The Old Testament, therefore, closes with the Jews back at their old home, with the temple restored, with the sacred writings gathered together, with the word of God being taught and with the voice of the living prophet still in the land. After this followed a somewhat varied history of about 400 years through all of which the light of the hope of the coming Messiah never died out.

Lessons of the Period. The discussions of the previous sections have brought out some of the significant teachings of this period, but the following statement of lessons will probably serve to stimulate thought. (1) God will use as his instruments others than his own people. See Cyrus and Artaxerxes. (2) God's work is both (a) constructive, as when he builds up, inspires, edicts and qualifies workers, and (b) destructive, as when he overcomes opposition. (3) A consecrated man is courageous and uncompromising, but none the less cautious. See Nehemiah. (4) There is a wise providence of God that includes all nations and displays perfect righteousness, perfect knowledge and perfect power. See the book of Esther, also the others. (5) Contentment may be false and harmful. See Hag. and Zech. (6) The comparative strength of the friends and enemies of a proposition does not determine the results. God must also be considered. (7) It pays to serve God. the Moral Governor of the world. See Mal. (8) The safety of a people demands that the marriage relation shall be sacredly regarded. (9) A rigid observance of the Sabbath is vital to the growth and well-being of a nation. (10) Mere forms of religion are displeasing to God unless accompanied by ethical lives. (11) Rules that oppress the poor court the Divine disfavor.

For Study and Discussion. (1) The lessons given in the last paragraph. (2) The decree of Cyrus. (3) The adversaries of Judah (Ezr. ch. 4; Neh. ch. 4), who they were and what they did. (4) The reforms of Ezra. (5) The reforms of Nehemiah. Compare them one by one with those of Ezra. (6) The traits of character of Ezra and Nehemiah. (7) Nehemiah's plan of work in rebuilding the temple. (8) The traits of character displayed by Vashti, Mordecai, Esther and Haman. (9) The Spirit of the return. Compare with the story of Ezra. Is. ch. 40, 48:20-21; Dan. 9:20; Ps. 137. Point out (a) the religious impulse, (b) the national pride, (c) the local attractions. (10) The rebuilding of the temple and of the wall. (11) The different sins rebuked by Malachi. (12) The kings of Babylon since Nebuchadnezzar, (b) [sic] The feast of Belshazzar, Dan. ch. 5, (c) The conquering of Babylon, (d) Organization of the kingdom under Darius, Dan. ch. 6, and of Ahasuerus, Esth.

Chapter XVII

From Malachi to The Birth of Christ.

No Scripture.

The Close of the Old Testament History. We now come to the close of Old Testament history and prophecy. Ezra and Nehemiah were at Jerusalem, one the governor and the other the priest of the people. Jerusalem and the temple had been restored and the worship of Jehovah re-established. This was about 445 B. C. and Judea was still under Persian rule. From this date to the opening of New Testament history, a period of about four hundred years, there are no inspired records. Neither prophet nor inspired historian is found among the Jews and there is no further development of revealed religion. It was, however, a period of vast importance and the history of the chosen people may be traced from secular sources. For convenience the history of the period may be divided into four sections: (1) The Persian Period. (2) The Greek Period. (3) The Period of Independence. (4) The Roman Period.

The Persian Period. The Persians continued their rule over Judea a little more than one hundred years after the close of Old Testament history. But in 332 B. C. Alexander the Great was enthroned over the monarchy, then under Darius, and inaugurated the era of Grecian supremacy. During this period, however, little happened in Palestine that was of much interest.

Under the Rule of the Greek Kings. Alexander the Great seemed to have formed a good opinion of the Jews and granted them many special favors. He regarded them as good citizens and gave them privileges as first class citizens of Alexandria and encouraged them to settle throughout his empire. Upon his death his kingdom was broken up into four kingdoms (Macedonia, Thrace. Syria and Egypt) and Judea was alternately under the rule of Syria and Egypt. All Palestine was permeated with the influence of the Greek language and philosophy. It was while Judea was under the rule of Ptolemy of Egypt that the

84

Septuagint version of the Old Testament was made. This made possible the reading of the Hebrew Scriptures in the Greek language and was one of the greatest missionary works of all times.

The Period of Independence. In 170 B.C. Antiochus Epiphiones began to oppress the Jews in an attempt to force them into idolatry and about 167 B.C. Judas Maccabeus began to lead a revolt which two years later was successful in throwing off the foreign yoke and establishing the independence of the Jews. They were now governed by a succession of rulers from the Maccabean family for a period of one hundred years. These rulers performed the double function of both civil and ecclesiastical head of the people. They were descendants of David and under their leadership Edom, Samaria and Galilee were added to their territory and much of the splendor and wealth of the golden days of the kingdom was restored.

The Roman Period. This period may be said to have begun in B.C. 63 and to have extended to A.D. 70. In B.C. 63 Pompey overran Palestine, destroyed Jerusalem and brought the Jews under Roman rule. By this conquest Jewish independence was forever lost. In B.C. 37 Herod the Great was appointed by the Roman emperor to the position of ruler of Palestine. In B.C. 20-18 he rebuilt the temple at Jerusalem, though it (all the buildings and walls) was not finished until many years after his death. He also built the temple of Samaria and continued to reign until Christ came and much longer.

The Entire Period. This entire period spans the time from the history of Nehemiah and the prophecy of Malachi to the coming of the Messiah. It opens with the Persian empire supreme and closes with Augustus Caesar as the head of Rome, the mistress of the world. When Jesus came Herod the Great governed Palestine and all the world was at peace.

The End of the Period. There are many points of view from which to study the conditions existing at the close of this period. But for our purpose it will probably suffice to consider (1) some signs of decadence or defects; (2) some hopeful signs. The facts touching these matters are to be gathered not only from secular history but from the life and work of Jesus as they are seen at work either for or against the progress of his work. (1) Unpropitious conditions. Among the signs of decadence or errors that needed correction should be noted: (a) There was a defective view of God. They regarded God as too far away; (b) They laid too much stress upon outward obedience and, thereby, left no place for motive in their service; (c) This led them to rest salvation upon a system of works and to multiply rules of obedience; (d) This led to too great demand for respect for the learned and of subordination to them; (e) The Jews thought that they had a special place in the salvation of God and as children of Abraham only felt the need of national deliverance. (2) Hopeful signs. Several conditions that bespeak good should be noted: (a) The Jews did have the truest conception of religion to be found anywhere in the world; (b) Their religion was a matter of deep concern to them and they showed an undying devotion to their religious institutions; (c) There was a keen sense of the worth of the individual; (d) There were many synagogues which led to a zeal to proselyte foreigners and opened the way for Gentile evangelism; (e) There was a widespread expectation of the Messiah whom the whole world could receive as its spiritual king; (f) The home life of the Jews was strongly religious and children were held in high esteem.

For Study and Discussion. (1) The career of Alexander the Great. (2) The reign of Ptolemy Soter and Ptolemy Philadelphus in Egypt. (3) The acts of Antiochus Epiphanes. (4) The story of Judas Maccabeus. (5) The story of the subjection of Judea to Rome. (6) The persecution of the Jews under the several rulers of the different countries to which they were subject during this period. (7) The religious parties of the period, especially the Pharisees and Sadducees.

Literature. The information necessary to understand these topics may be found in any one of the better Bible dictionaries, in Josephus and more or less in text books on Biblical history such as Blakie.

Chapter XVIII

From the Birth to The Ascension of Jesus.

The Four Gospels.

The Story of this Period. It is common to designate this period as the "Life of Christ," meaning the time he spent on earth. There is, however, no scripture life of Jesus. The gospels do not claim to present such a life. They do, however, give us a vast amount of material and though different in purpose and consequently in content, they do present the same general picture of Jesus. The matter of arranging the material in an orderly way presents much difficulty. If a topographical outline is attempted it can only be approximately correct because at some points the gospels leave us in uncertainty or in ignorance. If a chronological outline is attempted there is no less of uncertainty.

The following outline, however, may be accepted as a scheme of study for the period. (1) The childhood and youth of Jesus. From the birth of Jesus, B.C. 4 to the beginning of the ministry of John the Baptist, A.D. 26. (2) The beginning of Christ's ministry. From the beginning of John's ministry to Christ's first public appearance in Jerusalem, A.D. 27. (3) The early Judean ministry. From his first public appearance in Jerusalem to his return to Galilee, A.D. 27. (4) The Galilean ministry. From the return to Galilee to the final departure for Jerusalem, A.D., 29. (5) The Perean Ministry. From the departure from Galilee to the final arrival in Jerusalem, A.D. 30. (6) From the final arrival in Jerusalem to the resurrection, April, A.D. 30. (7) The forty days. From the resurrection to the ascension. May, A.D. 30.

The Childhood and Youth of Jesus. (1) The long preparation for his coming. The prophets had most emphatically proclaimed his coming and all things had from the beginning been divinely directed so that preparation might be made for his advent. His human ancestry had been selected and prepared. When the time drew near for him to appear, the coming of John the Baptist his forerunner, was announced to Zacharias his father (Lu. 1:5-25). This was quickly followed by the announcement of the birth of Jesus to Mary his mother (Lu. 1:26-38) and soon thereafter to Joseph, the espoused husband of Mary (Matt. 1:18-25). The beautiful story of his birth is told in the second chapter of Luke.

(2) The infancy. Of Jesus infancy we have several facts and incidents, (a) The appearance of the angels to the shepherds and the shepherds' visit to the babe, Lu. 2:8-20. (b) The circumcision at eight days old, Lu. 2:21. (c) The presentation in the temple where he was recognized by Simeon, Lu. 2:22-32. (d) The visit of the wise men (Matt. 2:1-12) and (e) The flight into Egypt, Matt. 2:13-23.

(3) His boyhood and youth. This is commonly called the years of silence: (a) We have the record of his parents' settlement in the city of Nazareth, Matt. 2:23; (b) We know that he had a normal growth, Lu. 2:40; (c) At twelve years old he was remarkably developed and from his reply to his mother we may infer that he was conscious of his mission, Lu. 2:41-50; (d) From Luke 2:50 we may infer something of the spirit which possessed him during the rest of his private life; (e) We also know his occupation (Mk.6:3).

The Beginning of Christ's Ministry. Here are several matters of importance. (1) The ministry of John the Baptist (Matt 3:1-12; Mk. 1:2-8; Lu. 3:1-18; John 1:6-33) who announced Christ's coming and prepared a people for him. This he did by preaching repentance and by baptising them as a profession of repentance and as a sign that they were forgiven. (2) The Baptism of Jesus. (Mt. 3:13-17; Mk. 1:9-11; Lu. 3:21-23; John 1:29-34.) At this time he put off the life of seclusion and entered upon his public career. He also received the Father's attestation to his sonship and the special equipment of the Holy Spirit for his work by which also John knew him to be the Messiah, John 1:33. By this act he also set the stamp of approval on John's work and showed that he was not in competition with John. (3) The temptation of Jesus (Mt. 4:1-11; Mk, 1:12-13; Lu. 4:1-13). We are given the place and length of time of this temptation, also three of the temptations and how they were met. In Heb. 2:18 and 5:18 we have some light on the purpose of this trial. It is probable, however, that all the import of it cannot be fully understood. (4) The work of Jesus begun. Here it is necessary to study two things: (a) The winning of his first six disciples (John 1:35-51); (b)

His first miracle (John 2:1-11). At this point it will also be of help to call to mind that the method of Jesus was to preach, teach and heal (Mt. 4:23). At the close of the marriage feast, which usually lasted six or seven days, Jesus went down to Capernaum (John 2:12).

The Early Judean Ministry. The records of this period are very brief and may be studied under three heads, (1) The incidents at Jerusalem during the first Passover of Christ's public ministry. The two principal incidents were the cleansing of the temple (John 2:13-22) and the conversation with Nicodemus, Jno. 3:1-31. (2) The work out in Judea, where he won and baptized many disciples, whereupon John was led to make testimony to Jesus at Aenon, John 3:22-36. (3) His successful work in Samaria, concerning which there is given the story of his message to the woman at the well and of his two days' stay at Sychar. The period is made notable by two of the greatest discourses of all his ministry: (a) that to Nicodemus; (b) that to the woman at Jacob's well.

The Gallilean Ministry. This is by far the longest and most important period of Christ's work. It is not wholly confined to Galilee. For during this time he certainly attends the feast at Jerusalem and also makes some excursions into the north country. If the study of the last period was embarrassed because of the scarcity of material, this one is all the more so because of the amount and variety of it. The following outline will, however, simplify the study. (1) The beginning of his work in Galilee. (Matt 4:12-25; 8:2-4, 14-17; 14:3-5. Mk. 1:14-45; 6:17-18; Lu. 4:14-3; 16; John 4:43-54). In this section we have the account of (a) John's imprisonment and of Christ's arrival in Galilee; (b) of the healing of the nobleman's son, and his settlement at Capernaum; (c) of the call of four fishermen and many miracles wrought at Capernaum; (d) of his first brief tour of Galilee.

(2) The antagonism of the scribes and Pharisees. (Matt 9:1-17, 12:1-14; Mk. 2:1-3:6; Lu. 5:17-6:11; John ch. 5). The more important matters of this record are: (a) The healing of the paralytic; (b) Matthew's call and feast; (c) the healing of the man at the pool of Bethsaida; (d) the story of the disciples in the grain fields and (e) the healing of the withered hand. In all these there is indicated the rising hostility to Jesus and his method, especially as regards his claim of power to forgive sins and in his attitude toward the despised classes and toward the Sabbath.

(3) The organization of his kingdom. (Matt. 12:15-21, 10:2-4; chs. 5-

7; Mk. 3:7-19; Lu. 6:2-49.) The fame of Jesus began to spread and it became necessary for him to create an organization to carry forward his work. This was done by calling out his twelve apostles and outlining to them the principles of his kingdom. This he did in the sermon on the mount.

(4) The second tour of Galilee. (Matt. 8:5-13; 11:2-30; Lu. 7:1-8:3.) The narration here gives the stories (a) of the Centurion's servant and the widow's son of Nain, (b) of John's last message and (c) of Jesus anointed by the sinful woman.

(5) His teachings and miracles by the Sea of Galilee. (Matt. 12:22-13:53, 8:23-34, 9:18-34; Mk. 3:19-5:43; Lu. 8:4-56.) In this section we have a large group of parables with their varied teachings and four very interesting miracles: (a) The stilling of the tempest; (b) The healing of the Gadarene demoniacs; (c) The story of Jainus' daughter; (d) Two dumb and a blind man.

(6) The third tour of Galilee. (Matt. 13:34-15:20, 9:35-11:1; Mk. 6:1-7:23; Lu. 9:1-17; John ch. 6.) Leaving Capernaum Jesus again came to his own city, Nazareth, where the people acknowledged the marvel of his wisdom and of his power but again rejected him-this time because of their knowledge of his lowly birth and unpretentious youth. Upon this rejection, Jesus and his disciples made another circuit amongst the cities and towns of Galilee. This tour is made notable by several incidents: (a) We have the sending out of the twelve on a tour of preaching, healing and raising the dead; (b) The story of the death of John the Baptist, who was the first New Testament person to suffer martyrdom for his conviction; (c) Two great miracles, that of feeding the five thousand and of walking on the sea; (d) Two great discourses of Jesus, that on "The Bread of Life" and on "Eating with unwashed hands."

(7) His first retirement into the north and return to the sea of Galilee. (Matt. 15:21-16:12; Mk. 7:24-8:26). Jesus went up into the coast of Tyre and Sidon where he healed the daughter of the Syrophoenician woman. On the return trip he passed through Decapolis where he healed a deaf and dumb man and performed many other miracles. After his return we have the record of the feeding of the four thousand, of his encountering the Pharisees about his authority and the story of the blind man of Bethsaida.

(8) The second retirement to the north and return to Capernaum. (Matt. 16:13-18 end; Mk. 8:27-9 end; Lu. 9:18-50). Jesus again journeys into the north and came into the parts of Caesarea Philippi where he drew from Peter the great confession, predicted his coming death, was transfigured before the favored three and healed the lunatic boy. On his return, as he neared Capernaum, he again foretold his death and resurrection and after he arrived at Capernaum, we have recorded the story of the coin in the fish's mouth and his discourse on humility, offenses and forgiveness.

(9) Jesus at the Feast of Tabernacles. (John chs. 7-8). By this time the joyous season of the Feast of Tabernacles drew near and his brothers, who though they did not believe in his deity, seemed to have some pride in him and urged him to go up among the people and make a display of his power. This he refused to do but went up secretly, probably with the hope of escaping the antagonism that was now being manifested toward him. There was, however, great excitement at Jerusalem concerning him and he found it necessary to go into the temple and boldly proclaim the teachings of his kingdom. These teachings may be studied under four heads: (a) The teaching of the first day and the division of the Jews concerning him; (b) The story of the adulterous woman; (c) His teaching concerning himself as the "Light of the World." He probably looked upon the great light over the treasury of the Lord's house which burned each night in commemoration of the cloud of fire that always guided and lighted Israel in the wilderness and was reminded of his own service for humanity and was prompted to this discourse; (d) His discourse on spiritual freedom and true children of Abraham.

The Perean Ministry. At the close of the Feast of Tabernacles Jesus returned to Galilee where he seems to have gathered around him a little company of loyal followers and made ready for his final departure to Jerusalem where he was to meat the death already foretold. The incidents of this period occurred during the journey. The material easily falls into three parts marking distinct sections of time. (1) From the departure from Jerusalem to the close of the Feast of Dedication. (Matt. 19:1-2, 8:18-22; Mk. 10:1; Lu. ch. 10; John ch.s 9-10). This is one of the most interesting sections of all and records several incidents of far-reaching importance: (a) The story of the healing of the man born

91

blind and the investigation of it by the Sanhedrin; (b) The story of the sending out of the seventy and their return is told. As the Lord's work drew near its close, he felt hat others should be sent out to do a like work to his own; (c) The story of the Good Samaritan and of his visit to Martha and Mary; (d) The allegory of the Good Shepherd; (e) The report of his visit to the Feast of Dedication.

(2) From the Feast of Dedication to the withdrawal to Ephraim. (Lu. 11:1-17:10; John 11:1-54). This section of the period is even more crowded with activity than was the former one. It is very difficult, therefore, to refer here to anything like all that is recorded of the period. Among The subjects discussed the following are the most important: (a) The true nature of prayer and the follies and hypocrisies of the Pharisees, Lu. ch. 11; (b) The danger of hypocrisy, of denying Christ, of covetousness and of the judgments of Christ, Lu. ch. 12; (c) The need and nature of repentance, the proper use of the Sabbath, the number that shall be saved and the fate of Jerusalem, Lu. ch. 13; (d) The law of conduct in the matter of feasts and counting the cost of discipleship, Lu. ch. 14; (e) Three parables of grace and two parables of warning, Lu. chs. 15-16; (f) Forgiveness and faith, Lu. 7:1-10; (g) The raising of Lazarus and withdrawal to Ephraim, John ch. 11.

(3) From the withdrawal to Ephraim to the final arrival at Jerusalem. (Matt. chs. 13-20; 26:8-13; Mk. ch. 10; 14:3-9; Lu. 17:11-19:28; John 11:55-12:11). This section is notable for the preponderance of teaching over the miracles reported. There are two miracles, that of healing ten lepers and the blind man of Jericho. The following show how large a place is given to teaching: (a) Concerning the coming of the kingdom; (b) concerning prayer, illustrated by the importunate widow and the Pharisee and publican; (c) Concerning divorce; (d) the blessing of little children; (e) the ambitions of James and John; (g) the visit to Zachaeus; (h) the parable of the pounds and the anointing of Jesus for burial.

The Final Ministry in Jerusalem. Of all the periods of the life of Christ this is the most significant. The gospels put most stress upon it and particularly upon his trial and death. The disciples soon learned to triumph in the cross, the seeming defeat out of which Jesus, through his resurrection, snatched victory. Everything recorded of this period has a ring of the tragical and seemed a preparation for the coming doom he was soon to meet. The material readily divides itself into three sections or periods. (1) From the final arrival in Jerusalem to the last hours of private intercourse with his disciples. (Matt. 21:11-26:16; Mk. chs. 11-13; 14: 1, 2, 10, 11; Lu. 19:29-22:6; John 12:12 end). Like every other section of his active ministry among the people this has in it some teachings and some miracles. The greatest act of all was, perhaps, the triumphal entry of Jesus into Jerusalem as king of the Jews. In this act he openly accepted the position of Messiah.

There is one important miracle, that of cursing and withering the fig tree. Some consider that a miraculous power was also used in the cleansing of the temple. The teachings may be grouped as follows: (a) The question about Christ's authority and his reply by question and the three parables of warning; (b) Three questions by the Jews and Christ's unanswerable question; (c) Seven woes against the scribes and Pharisees and the widow's mite; (d) The Gentiles seeking and the Jews rejecting Jesus; (e) a discourse on the destruction of Jerusalem and the end of the world; (f) the last prediction of his death and the conspiracy of Judas and the chief priests.

(2) Christ's last hours with his disciples. (Matt. 26:17-35; Mk. 14:12-31; Lu. 22:7 end; John chs. 13-17). Jesus has now withdrawn from the crowd and is alone with his disciples giving to them his final words of instruction and comfort. The whole of the material of this section seems to be surrounded by an atmosphere of sacredness that almost forbids our looking in upon its little company. This last evening that Jesus and the little group of disciples were together, is, however, so important that it is reported by the apostles. All the incidents of the evening seem to center around the institution of the last or Paschal Supper. But for the sake of study and as an aid to memory the events may be divided into three groups, (A) The supper. The order of events in connection with it seem to be: (1) the strife of the disciples for the place of honor; (2) the beginning of the Passover meal; (3) the washing of the disciples' feet; (4) the pointing out of the betrayer; (5) the departure of Jesus from the table; (6) the institution of the Lord's upper.

(B) The final instructions to the disciples. It is difficult to analyze these discourses. There are running through them one thread of teaching and one of comfort. In some sections one element seems to predominate and in other the other, To illustrate; chapters 13 and 15 of John seem to be more largely taken up with teaching, while chapters 14 and 16 have a larger element of words intended to comfort them. The effort seems to be to convince them that it is better for them for him to go away, that their spiritual fellowship with him would be more complete and their understanding and power more perfect because of the Comforter whom he would send.

(C) The final or intercessory prayer for them. With the close of this prayer, in which he prayed for their preservation, their preparation for service and their final union with him in his glory, and which he prayed that they might have fullness of joy (John 17:13) his ministry with them ended till after his death.

(3) Christ's suffering for the sins of the world. (Matt. 26:36-27 end: Mk. 14:32-15 end; Lu. 22:39-23 end; John chs. 18-19). From some good text on the Life of Christ or from the critical commentaries, the pupils can find a discussion of this section. The following outline will, however, be sufficient for our purpose here: (A) The agony in the garden and the betrayal and arrest. This picture of the suffering of soul experienced by the Savior in which he also yielded himself to the will of the Father stands out in blessed contrast against the weakness of his sleeping friends and the unspeakable criminality of the betrayer. Even in his arrest Jesus once more finds opportunity to show himself merciful in healing the ear of Malchus thereby, counteracting the injury caused by the folly or rashness of one of his friends.

(B) The Jewish trial. The order of this trial seems to have been somewhat as follows: (1) A preliminary trial before Annus; (2) A trial before day with only part of the Sanhedrin present; (3) A trial before the whole Sanhedrin at daybreak. Knowing his rights Jesus several times refused to act. (1) He refused to bear testimony because no legal charge had been made against him. (2) He refused to testify against himself which was within his right. (3) He demanded that they bring witnesses because that was just according to law. These last three points at which Jesus claimed and acted upon his rights instead of upon their request shows the tendencies of the trial to be unfair and illegal. If one understands the Jewish law of trial it will be easy to see how glaringly out of harmony with the law this trial was. There are at least ten illegalities in it.

(C) The Roman trial. This whole story abounds in evidences of the prejudice and moral degeneracy of the Jewish leaders. They hated

94

Roman rule past all words to tell and yet would pretend loyalty to Caesar to carry out their wicked purpose. By this means they put Pilate in a position that to release Jesus would make him appear to be untrue to Caesar in releasing one announced to be Caesar's enemy. The trial may be studied in the light of the different ones before whom he was tried. (1) The public and private examination before Pilate. (2) The examination before Herod. (3) The second examination before Pilate. This also was partly private and partly public. Again, following he outline of John, we may consider the events as they happened alternately outside and inside of the praetorium.

(D) The crucifixion. It would be difficult to exaggerate the cruelty and torture of crucifixion. "It was the most cruel and shameful of all punishments." The disciples, however, dwell most of all upon the shame of it. Such a death in the eyes of a Jew was the sign of the curse of God. Several things are of importance and should be remembered. (1) The throng that saw it. A few were friends, some were bitter enemies and many were curious on-lookers. Altogether there was a great crowd and Jesus was derided and mocked in his death. (2) The story of the two thieves who were crucified with Jesus and especially the conversion of the one who repented. (3) The seven sayings of Jesus while he is on the cross reveal his spirit and planning while undergoing this human outrage. They are worthy of careful study. (4) The miraculous occurrences of the day. There are three outstanding events that should be thought of as divine manifestations. They are: the darkness that covered the earth for three hours; the rending of the veil of the temple and the earthquake. The people were deeply moved by these marvelous signs. (5) The element of grace seen in it all. This is seen in the punishment of the innocent Jesus, while the guilty Barabbas went free; the saving of the guilty but penitent thief and several of the sayings of the cross.

(E) The burial and tomb. The burial was very hurried, lest they should break a Jewish law. Joseph of Arimathea and Nicodemus together took him from the cross and buried him and the officers made his grave as secure as possible and placed a guard over it. All this they did because of his saying that he would rise again in three days.

The Forty Days. (Matt. ch. 28; Mk. ch. 16; Lu. 23:56-24 end; John chs. 20-21; Acts 1:3-12; 1 Cor. 15:5-7.) It is hard to divide this period into sections in such a way as not to present many difficulties. The several events may, however, be grouped under the following heads. (1) The early morning. (2) The walk to Emmaus and appearance to Peter. (3) The appearance to the ten when Thomas is absent. (4) The appearance to the eleven, Thomas being present. (5) The appearance to seven disciples by the sea of Galilee. (6) Several other appearances mentioned by Paul. (7) The last appearance, when the commission was given and he ascended. The order of events as outlined cannot be assured with any certainty. Then, too, there are differences of detail as to the occurrences here outlined. Each of them, therefore, presents its own difficulties. The most perplexing of all these problems is the arrangement of the events of the resurrection morning and especially the movements of the various women mentioned.

Touching the whole resurrection problem all of the gospels agree upon several important matters: (1) In giving no description of the resurrection itself; (2) that the evidence of it began with the women's visit to the sepulcher in the early morning; (3) that the first sign was the removal of the stone; (4) that they saw angels before they saw the Lord; (5) that manifestations were granted to none but disciples; (6) that the disciples were not expecting such manifestations; (7) that at first they received these manifestations with hesitancy and doubt; (8) that these appearances were made to all kinds of witnesses, male and female, individuals and companies; (9) that they were so convinced of his resurrection and appearance to them that nothing could cause them to doubt it.

The resurrection was necessary to show that we had not a dead and suffering Christ but a living and triumphant one. "The ascension is the necessary completion of the resurrection" and is presupposed in all New Testament teaching. Jesus is everywhere thought of as having all power and is expected to return again from the presence of the Father with great glory.

Teachings of the Period. The most of the emphasis is put on the final teachings in connection with his death and resurrection. It may be well, however, to gather together a few truths touching his whole career. (1) Those concerning his humanity: (a) He grew and developed as any normal child; (b) His education and work was that of any normal person; (c) But the whole of his childhood was set in divine manifestations; (d) In life he showed all the effects of hunger, sorrow,

96

etc., found in any normal man. (2) Those concerning his super-human power. He exercised power over: (a) Physical nature; (b) sickness and physiological defects; (c) life and death; (d) demons and all spiritual powers; (e) over sin to forgive it. (3) Those found In his general teachings. There are many of these but the following are important to remember: (a) The truthfulness of the Old Testament scriptures; (b) The holiness and goodness and love of God; (c) The sinfulness of man and his need of salvation; (d) The value of repentance and faith as a means of bringing men into the favor of God; (e) His own duty and oneness with the Father; (f) The work and power of the Holy Spirit; (g) The purpose and work of his kingdom and church; (h) The power and nature of prayer; (i) The value of spiritual and the worthlessness of formal worship; (j) The true way to greatness through service.

(4) The teachings growing out of the crucifixion: (a) It proves that God will forgive; (b) It shows the great evil of sin; (c) It shows the need of cleansing before we can enter heaven; (d) It shows God's value of the soul; (e) It shows the value of salvation and the worth of eternal life; (f) It furnishes a motive to turn from sin that so offends God and endangers us; (g) It brings hope of forgiveness and cleansing.

(5) The teaching of the resurrection and ascension: (a) that Jesus is in truth God's son; (b) that there is another life; (c) that we shall also be resurrected; (d) that we shall know in the next life our loved ones of this life; (e) that our lives here have an influence and meaning beyond the grave.

For Study and Discussion. (1) Master all the material as given in this chapter, looking carefully into scripture references. (2) Study the geography of the country. (3) List all the divine manifestations in connection with the birth and childhood of Jesus. (4) Outline the entire career of John the Baptist, beginning with the vision to Zachariah before his birth. (5) Study in outline the sermon on the mount. (6) Find examples showing Christ's power exerted in each of the five directions suggested in "2" of "the teachings of the period" given above. (7) Discuss any outstanding events in the life of Jesus and his disciples that seem to members of the class to be epoch making in their influence. (8) Read and discuss Jesus' farewell addresses to his disciples. (9) Study carefully the scriptures covering the trial and crucifixion of Jesus. (10) Study the scriptures covering the period and outline further the events and teachings.

Chapter XIX

From the Ascension to The Church at Antioch.

Acts Chs. 1-12.

The Book of Acts. The book of Acts is the only purely historical book of the New Testament. It is as a continuation of the gospel of Luke. It follows the fortunes of the infant church and gives us all the light we have in regard to its further organization and development, but it does not claim to be a complete history of the work of the early church. As a history it is as remarkable for what it omits as for what it narrates. The central theme is the triumph and progress of the gospel in spite of all the opposition and persecution which its advocates met. The chief purpose seems to be to show the progress of Christianity among the Gentiles and only so much of the work among the Jews is given as will authenticate the other. The whole book falls into three sections: (1) The church at work in Jerusalem, chs. 1-7. (2) The church at work in Palestine, chs, 8-12. (3) The church at work among the Gentiles, chs. 13-28.

The material of the period which we are now to study includes the first two points and should be read in connection with the following outline:

I. The church at work in Jerusalem, chs. 1-7.

1. Preparation for witnessing, 1:1-2:4. Under this there is given: (1) Christ's last instructions and ascension and (2) The church in the upper room including the election of Matthias and the coming of the Holy Spirit.

2. The first witnessing. Here are given 2:5-47: (1) The first witnessing, (2) the first message, (3) the first fruit of the witnessing.

3. The first persecution 3:1-4:31. Here we have the first persecution and the occasion for it.

4. The Blessed state of the church, 4:32-5 end There is great love and unity and God indorses their work by the destruction of Ananias and his wife and by the release of apostles from prison.

5. The first deacons, 6:1-7.

6. The first martyr 6:8-7 end.

II. The church at work in Palestine, chs. 8-12.

1. Witnesses scattered, 8:1-4.

2. Philip witnesses in Samaria and Judea, 8:5-40.

3. The Lord wins new witnesses, 9:1-11:18. (1) Saul. (2) Aeneas, etc. (3) Dorcas, Mary, etc. (4) Cornelius.

4. Center of labor changed to Antioch, 11:19 end.

5. The witnesses triumph over Herod's persecution, ch. 12.

The Principle Events of this Period. Many things which on the surface seem to be of little importance, contributed much toward shaping the destiny of the early church. The following, however, should be remembered as the great outstanding events of the time. (1) The ascension with the incidents connected with it. (2) The Baptism of the Holy Ghost with the consequent sermon of Peter and its results. (3) The first persecution of the Apostles, with Peter's sermon and the measures taken by the Sanhedrin to stop the movement. (4) The punishment of Ananias and his wife. (5) The appointment of the first deacons. (6) The martyrdom of Steven. (7) The work of Philip in Samaria and the conversion of the Eunuch. (8) The conversion of Saul of Tarshish. (9) The conversion of Cornelius with connected events. (10) The church's acknowledgement of the validity of this work among the Gentiles, Acts 11:18. (11) The great work at Antioch. (12) The martyrdom of James and the death of Herod.

The Organization and Control of the Early Church. Jesus had set up his church and left it his final commission. Its organization was a matter of growth and was increased only as new conditions arose that made it necessary to the success and efficiency of their work. They elected, at the suggestion of Peter, Matthias to take the place of Judas as one of their witnesses. When conditions arose that threatened the success of their work, they elected deacons to assist the apostles in caring for the more temporal work of the church. In it all it is clear that the church as a whole transacted the business. The Apostles no doubt had a very good influence but did not assume to dictate to the church what did not "please the whole multitude" (Acts 6:5). All responsibility was put upon the church as a democratic and self-governing body.

The Persecutions of the Church. In the persecutions which Jesus suffered the Pharisees took the lead, but the opposition met by the early disciples was led by the Sadducees. This was because of the doctrine of the resurrection, preached by the apostles. The persecutions deepened and widened very rapidly. (1) They were given public hearing, commanded not to teach in Jesus' name and after threatening were let go. (2) They were released without punishment only by the appeal of Gamaliel, a doctor of the law. (3) On account of the universal aspect of Christianity, preached by Steven, the Pharisees joined the Sadducees in opposing the Christians and their joint persecution led to the death of Steven and the scattering of the disciples from Jerusalem, 6:8-8:3. (4) The Romans who for the most part had been indifferent to the movement also joined the Sanhedrin in the attempt to suppress the brethren. Accordingly Herod Agrippa, hoping to gain the good will of the Jews, seized the apostle James and put him to death and seeing that this made him popular seized Peter and would have destroyed him but for divine intervention.

In spite of all this persecution these early Christians made wonderful progress. They were unmoved in their purpose to establish their faith. They went everywhere preaching the gospel of the kingdom. They openly declared that they would not refrain from preaching what they conceived to be their duty to God. They boldly threw their doctrine into the teeth of their antagonists. Such courage was something new in the history of the Jews. They even "rejoiced that they were counted worthy to suffer dishonor for his name."

Their Growth and Influence. The courage already mentioned could not fail to bear fruit. The second chapter tells of three thousand, added to them in one day and then of others day by day. In chapter five it is said a multitude of believers both men and women added to them. Chapter six says that "the disciples multiplied in Jerusalem exceedingly; and a great company of the priests were obedient to the faith." The priests were for the moat part Sadducees and the fact that many of these who had been active in arresting the disciples now came to accept their teaching is highly significant touching the matters of their success.

Extension of the Gospel to the Gentiles. One of the most interesting topics for study found in the records of this period is the way in which Christians gradually extended into the borders of the Gentiles. Many questions were raised that had to be solved-questions that had not been before raised among the followers of Jesus. (1) Philip went into Samaria and many of these half-bred Jews believed. Here he was following the steps of Jesus who had also met with success and introduced his teachings before going outside to those in no wise akin to the Jews. (2) Peter and John were sent to Samaria and not only approved the work of Philip but bestowed upon these Samaritans the Holy Spirit and themselves preached to many Samaritan villages. (3) Peter made a tour of certain Judean villages and came down to Joppa where he lodged with a tanner and would, according to Jewish law, have been unclean. This tends to show that he was coming to see that the ceremonial distinctions of the Levites were not so binding. (4) Peter preached to Cornelius a Gentile and he and his household received the Holy Ghost and baptism and spake with tongues. (5) Having heard Peter's explanation of his course the church glorified God and acknowledged that God had granted repentance and life to the Gentiles. (6) Paul the chosen vessel to bear the Gospel to the Gentiles was saved. (7) The work spread to Antioch of Syria and Barnabas was sent to investigate it and soon went to Cilicia and brought Paul to Antioch and the two labored there a year, then made a visit to Jerusalem to carry gifts to the poor and returned to Antioch bringing John Mark. This period closes with them still at Antioch.

The Teachings of this Period. (1) Men can succeed in any right cause in spite of opposition. (2) Popularity is not required to give one success as a Christian work. (3) Small numbers are not a sign of weakness and do not foretoken defeat. (4) The gospel truth, courageously preached, can win its way into the hardest hearts. (3) Consciousness of duty, divinely imposed is the most powerful stimulus to action.

For Study and Discussion. (1) The Great Commission, ch. 1. (2) Peter's sermon on the day of Pentecost. (3) Stephen's address of defense. (4) The liberality of these Christians or their provision for the poor. (5) The place of prayer in the work of these disciples. (6) The references to the Holy Spirit and his work. (7) The teachings of the period concerning Jesus. (8) Concerning the resurrection. (9) All the events, persecutions, teachings, etc., mentioned above.

Chapter XX

From Antioch to The Destruction of Jerusalem.

Acts 13-28 and all the rest of the New Testament except the epistles of John and Revelation.

The Changed Situation. We have now come to a turning point in the whole situation. The center of work has shifted from Jerusalem to Antioch, the capital of the Greek province of Syria, the residence of the Roman governor of the province. We change from the study of the struggles of Christianity in the Jewish world to those it made among heathen people. We no longer study many and various persons and their labors but center our study upon the life and labors of Paul.

The Divine Call. Certain prophets of the church at Antioch were engaged in solemn prayer and worship when the Holy Spirit instructed them to send Paul and Barnabas to do the work to which they were called. Here, then, the Holy Spirit takes charge of the movement. He inaugurates, directs and promotes this work. When the call came it is probable that Paul had but little idea of the magnitude of the work which he was to do. He was not aware that his work and teaching would change the religion and philosophy of the whole world.

The Time and Extent of Paul's Journeys. The most of his work was accomplished during three great missionary journeys. The time occupied for these great journeys with the distance traveled has been estimated as follows: the first journey 1400 miles and three years; the second journey 3200 miles and three years; the third journey 3500 miles and four years; or a total of 8100 miles representing ten years of labor. To this must be added his journey to Rome which required a whole winter and was about 2300 miles and many side trips of which we have no record. It is also commonly thought that he was released at the end of two years at Rome and again entered upon mission work that probably lasted four years and carried him again into Macedonia, Asia Minor, Crete and Spain.

The First Missionary Journey. (Acts, chs. 13-14). The company consisted of Saul and Barnabas and John Mark. They went by way of the isle of Cyprus and at Paphos the capital of the island the governor was converted and Saul was afterward called Paul. They reached Pamphylia and Pisidia in Asia. John Mark left them in Pamphylia and returned home. In the cities of Pisidia Paul was persecuted and opposed. At Antioch he made a complete break with the Jews and at Lystra they stoned him until they thought he was dead. From Derbe the missionaries retraced their steps except that they did not go through Cyprus on the return to Antioch. Their stay at Antioch was marked by an important church council at Jerusalem, Acts 15:1-35. At this council it was decided that Gentile Christians were not bound by the requirement of the Jewish law. This decision was instrumental in determining that Christianity was not simply a new branch of Judaism but was a new religion.

Second Missionary Journey. (Acts. 15:36-18:22). Paul proposed that he and Barnabas visit the brethren in every city "where he had already preached," but he declined to yield to the wish of Barnabas to take Mark with them and in consequence separated from Barnabas. He took Silas and went overland through Syria and Cilicia to the scene of his former labors. At Lystra he was joined by Timothy. He was restrained by the Holy Spirit from further work in Asia and called into Europe by the "Macedonian call" while at Troas. While in Europe he labored at several places, the most conspicuous service being rendered at Philippi, Thessalonica and Corinth. Strong churches grew up at each of these places to which he later wrote letters. He returned to Antioch by way of Ephesus where he spent a little time, and Caesarea, from whence he probably visited Jerusalem.

While on this Journey during his long stay at Corinth Paul wrote First and Second Thessalonians and probably the book of Galatians also. If the time to be devoted to this course will allow, these epistles should be read at this point. The author's The Bible Book by Book will furnish an outline guide for such reading.

Third Missionary Journey. (Acts. 18:33-21:17). How long Paul remained at Antioch at the close of the second journey is not known. But when he had finished his visit he set out again to revisit some of the places formerly touched and to cultivate some new fields. The outline and work of this journey may be put down as follows: (1) He passes through Galatia and Phrygia strengthening the disciples. (2) His work of nearly three years at Ephesus. (3) The trip through Macedonia and Greece. (4) The return trip through Macedonia to Jerusalem. Luke seems to desire to narrate only what is new and most important. He, therefore, goes fully into the work at Ephesus. (1) There was the incident of the work of Apollos and the baptism of some of John's disciples. (2) Three months work among the Jews. (3) Two years of teaching in the school of Tyrannus. (4) A "season" after he sent Timotheus and Etastus into Macedonia. The success of this work is seen especially in two incidents. (1) The burning of the books of the Jewish exorcists which were valued at over $31,000. (2) The checking of the sale of images of the idol, Diana, which resulted in a great tumult.

After this tumult at Ephesus Paul departed into Macedonia and seems to have visited the principal cities and finally arrived at Corinth where a plot to kill him was formed. Upon discovering this plot he set out on his return trip to Jerusalem, going back through Macedonia. This trip is notable for several things. (1) The seven days stay at Troas which was significant because of an all night service and the accident to Eutychus. (2) The conference at Miletus with the Elders of Ephesus in which he reviewed his work among them and indicated to them that they would see him no more. (3) A week's stay at Tyre where he was persuaded not to go to Jerusalem. (4) Many days spent at Caesarea during which Agabus, who had formerly told them of the coming drouth, predicted that the Jews of Jerusalem would bind Paul and deliver him to the Gentiles. (5) The arrival at Jerusalem where he was kindly received by James and the elders.

This journey also was marked by the writing of some of Paul's most notable epistles. (1) The First Letter to the Corinthians. He wrote this letter while at Ephesus just before leaving for Macedonia. (2) The Second Letter to the Corinthians. After Paul came into Macedonia he met Titus with tidings from the Corinthians whereupon he wrote them this second letter, probably from Philippi. (3) The Letter to the Romans. From Macedonia Paul went into Achaia where he stayed three months and while staying with Gaius in Corinth (Rom. 16:23; 1 Cor. 1:14) he wrote this great epistle. The occasion, purpose, outline and other information concerning these epistles may be found in The Bible Book by Book.

At Jerusalem. Although Paul was received kindly by the brethren and although he took a certain precaution that he might not offend the many thousands of Jews that were in Jerusalem at the feast, some Asiatic Jews saw him and raised a great tumult. (1) They began to beat him and he would no doubt have been killed had he not been rescued by Roman soldiers. (2) As a prisoner he was being borne to the Tower of Antonia, but on the stairway asked and obtained permission to speak to the angry Jews. (3) When they would no longer hear him he was removed to the castle and ordered scourged. He saves himself from this by claiming his Roman citizenship. (4) He was brought before the Jewish Sanhedrin which he threw into confusion by expressing his belief in the resurrection and afterwards was put in prison. (5) On account of the plot to kill him which was discovered by Paul's nephew he was sent away under heavy guard to Caesarea.

Paul at, Caesarea. When Paul reached Caesarea he was under Roman jurisdiction. He was allowed some privileges. The most important incidents of this two years' imprisonment may be put down somewhat as follows. (1) His trial before Felix during which he was prosecuted by Tertullus and he himself made a speech of defense. (2) His second hearing before Felix, no doubt in private, with his wife Drusilla after which he held him in the hope that he would bribe Felix. (3) His trial before Festus during which he claimed his right as a Roman citizen and appealed to Caesar. (4) He had a hearing before Festus and King Agrippa II during which Paul spoke.

Paul's Six Last Addresses. In connection with the story of Paul in Jerusalem and Caesarea we have preserved for us six of his last addresses. In the light of his imprisonment and eminent danger they show his great faith and courage and are given here for study. (1) His Speech before the Jewish Mob, Acts 21:1-29. (2) His speech before the Jewish council. Acts 22: 30-23:10. (3) His speech before Felix. Acts 24:10-22. (4) His speech before Felix and his wife Drusilla, Acts 24:24-27. (5) His speech before Festus, Acts 25:7-11. (6) His speech before Festus and King Aggrippa II, Acts 26:1-32.

Paul's Journey to Rome. Paul now takes up his long journey to Rome. The voyage consumes most of the winter and three ships are used to convey him. (1) From Caesarea to Myra, a city of Lycia. Their ship touched at Sidon where Paul was allowed to visit his friends. (2)

From Myra to the Island of Malta. On this voyage they touched at Fair Havens, tried to reach Phenice and had fourteen days of storm. (3) They were cast the island of Malta, where they spent three months. (4) The journey completed to Rome, going by way of Syracuse, Rhegium, Puteoli, Apii Forum and Three Taverns.

Paul at Rome. The Roman Christians came out to meet him at Apii Forum, forty-three miles from Rome. Several things should be noticed. (1) Paul after three days explained his situation to the Jews and planned another day when he would further address them. (2) Next he turned to the Gentiles and taught them. (3) He hired (rented) a house and for two years had liberty of speech and taught whoever would come to him. The story of Acts closes here, but it is commonly believed that Paul was released and visited Spain and Asia and later was rearrested and brought to Rome again where he was put to death.

The Epistles of this Period. The epistles written during this period may be divided into two groups: (1) Those written by Paul; (2) Those written by others. Those written by Paul are the following: (1) Philippians, Ephesians, Colossians and Philemon. All of these were written from Rome during Paul's first imprisonment at Rome and would come in the years 62 and 63 A.D. (2) First Timothy and Titus. These were probably written in Macedonia about A.D. 66. This is on the supposition that Paul was released from the imprisonment at Rome and made other preaching tours. (3) Second Timothy. This was written from the Roman prison just before his death about A.D. 67 or 68. This would have been a second imprisonment and we know nothing of this except by tradition. (4) Hebrews. There are many eminent scholars who think some other than Paul wrote this book, but it is put down here because it was so long and so unanimously considered his and because the point against his authorship does not seem fully established. It was written some time before A.D. 70, as the temple and its worship were still in force.

There are four other letters of the period. (1) The Epistle of James. This epistle was probably written about A.D. 50 but some think it was written as late as A.D. 62 and it is put in for consideration here because of the uncertainty. (2) The First Epistle of Peter, which was written about A.D. 66. (3) The Second Epistle of Peter, written about A.D. 67 and certainly before the fall of Jerusalem. (4) The Epistle of Jude, written about A.D. 66. The Bible Book by Book will furnish the student with a statement concerning the occasion, purpose, outline of contents and other introductory discussions.

Lessons of the Period. (1) One man with proper consecration can be a blessing to all the world. (2) The same teaching sometimes wins one and repels another. (3) The fact that one is divinely led does not guarantee that one may not be wrongly treated by men. (4) Persecution can not destroy one's happiness if one is conscious of doing the will of God. (5) Strategic centers are the most fruitful fields of mission work. (6) False religious beliefs are less tolerant than the true. (7) God may save a whole company for the sake of one man. (8) No matter what calamity comes to us we may in the midst of it be a source of blessing to others.

For Study and Discussion. (1) The countries visited by Paul. Draw maps and indicate his journeys. (2) The history and importance of the principal cities visited by him (make a list of them and consult the Bible dictionaries). (3) Paul's companions in the work (make a list of them and consult the Bible dictionaries). (4) The Apostle Paul himself: (a) His birth and childhood; (b) his education; (c) his conversion. (5) The persecutions of Paul. (6) The miraculous or superhuman element seen in this section. (7) The value of the Roman citizenship to Paul. (8) Paul's letters: (a) Name them and tell where in these journeys each comes in; (b) learn something of the occasion, purpose and outline of each. (9) The other epistles of this period. (10) The time and extent of Paul's journeys. (11) The church council at Jerusalem. (12) The Roman officers met in this narrative-what sort of men, etc. (13) Paul's speeches as given here.

Chapter XXI

Destruction of The Temple to The Death of The Apostle John.

Epistles of John and Revelation.

The Period of History. This period begins with the fall of the city of Jerusalem, A.D. 70, and ends with the death of John, the last of the apostles. We have but little scripture touching the conditions of this period. Indeed, all of it is inferential so far as the scripture is concerned. We may, however, learn much from secular history and tradition.

The Destruction of Jerusalem. Jesus had predicted the fall of this beloved city. Many frightful massacres of Jews had occurred in Judea before the end of the last period, but it was in A.D. 70, about two years after Paul's death, that Titus destroyed Jerusalem and the temple and Judaism had its downfall. After this the marks of separation between Christianity and Judaism became more and more distinct. From that time the Jewish religion has never gained ascendancy in any country.

From A.D. 70 to A.D. 100. The general history of this period has in it little of interest. At the end of the very creditable reign of emperor Vespasian, who was on the throne of Rome when Jerusalem fell, Titus, called "The delight of the human race," reigned in his stead. During his reign occurred that awful eruption of Vesuvius that buried Pompeii. Titus was succeeded by his brother Domitian, who was one of the greatest tyrants that ever ruled in any country. It is generally supposed that John was banished to the Isle of Patmos during the reign of Domitian. After Domitian reigned Nerva and Trojan, the last of which showed great talent and brought back much of the early vigor to the empire. The cyclopedias and histories of Rome will give information about the period.

The Literature of the Period. The history of the Christians in this period is very obscure because of the scanty literature produced in it. What literature we have of these years may be divided into two classes:

(1) Scripture books. These are the three epistles of John, which were written at Ephesus a while before his banishment, probably about 80 or 85 A. D., and the Revelation, which was composed while in exile on Patmos about 95 or 96 A. D. (2) Some early Christian writings not included in the canon of the New Testament. Of this class of writings is the Epistle of Clement of Rome to the Corinthians, written about 96-98 A.D., and the Epistle of Barnabas and the Teaching of the Twelve Apostles, probably written sometime before A.D. 100. This then is a period of transition from the Canonical to the Patristic literature.

Death of John and End of Scripture History. John was on the Isle of Patmos as an exile because of his testimony for Jesus. He seems to have lived until the end of the first century and is said to have met death in a cauldron of boiling oil. The last of the apostles being now dead the canon of the scripture is closed and the power of miracles removed and Christianity left to win its own way by means of the efforts and the prayers of the disciples and the grace which God ordinarily grants to them. Thus ends the scripture history-with a completed revelation and the Christian churches set up as a witness for Christ.

Lessons of the Period. It is difficult to draw, from a period of which we know so little, any certain conclusions. We are perhaps safe in making some observations. (1) Christianity must always make its way against opposition. (2) The Christian faith gives courage and joy in the most trying circumstances. (3) Christianity will finally triumph over its enemies.

For Study and Discussion. (1) From the Bible dictionaries, cyclopedias, etc., study the reigns of the different Roman emperors of this period. (2) Learn something of the nature and contents of the Patristic literature mentioned in this discussion. (3) The four New Testament books of this period.

9 781604 448436